NARCISSISTIC PARENTS

The Complete Guide for Adult Children

This Book Includes the Best of

Narcissistic Mothers
How to Handle a Narcissistic Parent and Recover from CPTSD

&

Narcissistic Fathers
How to Deal with a Toxic Father and Complex PTSD

Caroline Foster

Copyright © 2019-2021

All rights reserved. No portion of this book may be reproduced, stored in a retrieval system, or transmitted in any form or by any means - electronic, mechanical, recording, or otherwise - except for brief quotations in printed reviews without the prior written permission of the publisher or the author. Excerpt from the book "Narcissistic Partner Abuse: Change Yourself to Stop Being a Victim" reprinted by permission.

Disclaimer

The information contained within this document is for educational and entertainment purposes only. All effort has been executed to present accurate, up-to-date, and reliable, complete information. No warranties of any kind are declared or implied.

Readers acknowledge that the author is not engaging in the rendering of legal, financial, medical, or professional advice. The content within this book has been derived from various sources. Please consult a licensed professional before attempting any techniques outlined in this book. Under no circumstances will any blame or legal responsibility be held against the publisher or author for any damages, reparation, or monetary loss due to the information contained within this book, either directly or indirectly.

Download the Audiobook Version of this Book

for FREE

Just by Signing Up for a FREE 30-Day Audible Trial

Scan the QR Code Below!

Table of Contents

AUTHOR'S NOTE 9

INTRODUCTION 11

PART ONE RECOGNIZING THE PROBLEM 13

1.1 What is Pathological Narcissism 13

1.2 Inside the Mind of a Narcissist 16

1.3 Types of Narcissism 18

1.4 Narcissistic Strategies of Manipulation 22

1.5 Pathological Narcissists as Parents 30

1.6 Signs of Narcissistic Parenting 32

1.7 Enablers 39

PART TWO NARCISSISTIC MOTHERS 43

2.1 The Narcissistic Mother and the Roles She Chooses for Her Children 46

2.2 Types of Narcissistic Mothers 57

2.3 Narcissistic Mothers and Their Sons 62

2.4 Narcissistic Mothers and Their Daughters 70

PART THREE NARCISSISTIC FATHERS 75

3.1 The Narcissistic Father and the Roles He Chooses for His Children 76

3.2 Types of Narcissistic Fathers 85

3.3 Narcissistic Fathers and Their Sons 87

3.4 Narcissistic Fathers and their Daughters 95

PART FOUR SOLUTIONS 101

4.1 Effects of Narcissistic Abuse on Adult Children 101

4.2 How to Handle a Narcissistic Parent 106

4.3 Protect Yourself from Narcissistic Parents 111

4.4 Protect Yourself from Gaslighting 117

4.5 How to Outsmart the Narcissistic Double Bind Strategy 120

4.6 Taking Back Your Power 122

4.7 Move Out from a Toxic Environment: Practical Tips 125

4.8 Caring for an Aging Narcissistic Parent 128

PART FIVE HEALING 131

5.1 Complex Post-Traumatic Stress Disorder (CPTSD) 131

Emotional Flashbacks 131

Toxic Shame 135

Self-abandonment 138

Inner critic 142

Social anxiety 144

5.2 Self-healing Tips 150

CONCLUSIONS 153

AUTHOR'S NOTE

I WRITE BOOKS FOR PEOPLE who are dealing with narcissists in different situations. I don't write to display my knowledge or to brag about my credentials. My books are simple and do not contain bibliographic references because victims of narcissistic abuse are not interested in academic works. They simply recognize the truth while reading it since they have experienced the topics of these books throughout their lives.

Dear victim of narcissistic abuse, I care about you, and even if you cannot heal simply by reading a book, I hope that my work will make a positive difference in your life. This is my ambition, and I wish you all the best.

If you want to support my work, you can leave your honest review.

INTRODUCTION

THIS BOOK IS A FUSION OF TWO BOOKS: Narcissistic Mothers (How to Handle a Narcissistic Parent and Recover from CPTSD) and Narcissistic Fathers (How to Deal with a Toxic Father and Complex PTSD). Rather than simply putting the content of two books one after the other, I decided to merge them into a coherent volume, eliminating redundant content.

This book provides a complete picture of narcissistic parenting, analyzing all possible situations. Indeed, the consequences of narcissistic abuse on adult children of narcissistic parents change depending on different situations. For example, the role assigned by narcissistic parents to their children causes different outcomes in adulthood. The golden child is the most exposed to becoming a pathological narcissist, and the lost child is more likely to develop addictions and end up in prison. The scapegoat will likely become a victim of narcissistic partners in adulthood.

Part Four and Five are full of advice and tips to handle your narcissistic parents and start healing from narcissistic abuse. Even if only a good psychotherapist can successfully treat a traumatized adult child of a narcissistic parent, this book contains the complete information available and concrete effective advice to contrast CPTSD symptoms.

My aim is that, reading this book, you will understand how it's possible to heal after a life of narcissistic abuse.

PART ONE
RECOGNIZING THE PROBLEM

1.1 What is Pathological Narcissism

LET'S START WITH THIS: Narcissism is a mental illness, and only a qualified mental health professional can diagnose a person with Narcissistic Personality Disorder (NPD). Ordinary people don't have an accurate picture of the issue. They only use the word "narcissist" as a label based on their limited knowledge of the subject, what they have heard from others, seen on the Internet, or personally experienced. Therefore, it's important to understand what narcissism is and isn't.

You cannot diagnose a personality disorder by just reading search engine result pages. Narcissism is a psychological affliction that has different levels, and professionals use various tests to determine where a person falls on the narcissism spectrum. Despite all these tests, it's still difficult to officially diagnose a person with NPD.

The Diagnostic and Statistical Manual of Mental Disorders, published by the American Psychiatric Association, provides professional information on identifying a person with pathological narcissism. This book, also known as the Bible of Psychiatry, explains that to be diagnosed with Narcissistic Personality Disorder (NPD), a person has to meet at least five of the following criteria:

- Has a grandiose sense of self-importance; for example, exaggerates achievements and talents, expects to be recognized as superior.

- Has fantasies of unlimited success, power, brilliance, beauty, or idyllic love.

- Believes that they are "special" and should only associate with other "special" or high-status people or institutions.

- Requires excessive admiration.

- Has a sense of entitlement, that is, an unreasonable expectation of favorable treatment, or automatic compliance with their wishes.

- Takes advantage of others to achieve their ends.

- Lacks empathy and is unwilling or unable to recognize other people's feelings or needs.

- Is often envious of others and believes that others are envious in return.

- Shows arrogant, haughty behaviors or attitudes.

Let's see how these criteria can be applied to recognize narcissists in everyday life. **Narcissism is not selfishness**. People often confuse narcissism with self-love, contentment, being inconsiderate, opinionated, and attention-loving. The problem is that, from time to time, all of us naturally exhibit these kinds of behaviors.

Are we all narcissists? Of course not! The fact that someone exhibits one or two of these traits does not make that person a narcissist. Misinformation like this on the Internet waters down the true meaning of pathological narcissism, which is more than just traits or moods.

Pathological narcissists will constantly try to erode their victim's will to live. They are like cancer.

Since narcissism occurs on a spectrum, it takes a combination of several factors to know where a person falls on this continuum. While all narcissists tend to be abusive in one way or another, it isn't accurate to label every abuser as a narcissist. For this reason, recognizing abusive tendencies is not enough to identify a narcissist. We must look at their everyday life, which is also heavily affected by their condition.

What should you pay attention to? NPD is technically known as a Cluster B personality disorder. Therefore, to understand more accurately the person you are dealing with, it may be helpful to know more about disorders in Cluster B. People in this cluster often struggle to regulate their feelings, are over-emotional, erratic, dramatic, and sometimes unpredictable.

They also have impaired relationships, are incapable of intimacy, and find it difficult to maintain long-term relationships. People with a Cluster B personality disorder may also find it hard to understand themselves and have difficulties relating to others.

For a proper diagnosis of NPD to be made, these symptoms have to cause day-to-day problems with a person's functioning or behavior.

1.2 Inside the Mind of a Narcissist

Now, let's analyze what goes on in the mind of a narcissist.

"I am the best."

One prominent behavior of pathological narcissists is an inflated sense of self - the big ego, the idea that everything and everyone should revolve around them. For this reason, narcissists feel naturally entitled to special privileges and have very poor boundaries when it comes to relating to others. Usually, they have very little regard for etiquette or protocol, expect to be treated as special, and want you to see, notice, and even worship them for their achievements. A pathological narcissist may also exhibit arrogance, which is often nothing more than deep-seated fear.

"I can't be wrong."

Narcissists are not easily influenced by day-to-day experiences like you and me. Life experiences come with ups and downs, and these often help us become more emotionally and psychologically mature. We gain a more realistic view of life, of how it works, and we understand what to expect and not to expect. Narcissists, however, have an inflated sense of self and are resistant to admitting that they could be wrong. Instead, they will project their failures onto others. Beneath the narcissist's facade of arrogance and self-aggrandizement is a feeling of emptiness and a lack of introspection.

"You should be like me."

When relating to others, narcissists use the same strategy with different people. They are often very good at putting people on a pedestal.

They overvalue you - and devalue you just as quickly. You might be humiliated and treated in a passive-aggressive fashion and even abused. For this reason, most narcissists are domestic abusers.

Narcissists view others as an extension of themselves. They see people as their mirror image. If you are smart and beautiful and clever, they are attracted to you and idealize you. But as soon as you disagree with them or do something that they don't want you to do, they become quickly disappointed and often try to put you down.

They cannot understand that people might have a different point of view, or have their own life, or live in a different way from what they consider correct. The narcissist is good at devaluing others.

1.3 Types of Narcissism

Although narcissism exists on a spectrum, there are two major subcategories of NPD: Overt and Covert Narcissism.

Overt/Grandiose Narcissism

The overt or grandiose narcissist displays very clearly an over-inflated sense of self. They consider themselves extremely brilliant and have a high sense of superiority. In their relationships with others, they dominate and exploit. They fiercely compete with others and are intensely aggressive, seeking to ascend any hierarchy in the shortest amount of time possible. Eventually, they banish you by treating you condescendingly or as if you didn't exist.

Overt narcissists often display their emotions, show excitement, and can even be charming. They can't cope with boredom and are not capable of deep mental introspection. They display anger at the slightest resistance, particularly if they don't get their way. They are also jealous. Overt narcissists are extroverts, approaching people easily, and bursting full of energy. At times, they are also impulsive, take lots of risks, have low self-awareness, and always look for the shortest way to get what they want while looking good doing it.

Overt narcissists display clearly and evidently their grandiosity, which is the staple trait of NPD.

Covert Narcissism

In covert narcissists, also known as vulnerable or shy narcissists, the sense of grandiosity is less evident. This does not necessarily mean that covert narcissists consciously try to hide their narcissistic behavior.

Rather, they do not have the personality structure that makes their condition visible. Unlike grandiose narcissists, covert narcissists present themselves sometimes as superior, while other times as inferior. Covert narcissists behave in very subtle ways. They are often self-referencing but can appear painfully sensitive. They are hurt by criticism and don't do well with insults.

Covert narcissists don't rapidly ascend the hierarchy because they are very sensitive to criticism, which instills a sense of unfulfillment in their minds. Their inferiority is easily triggered, and they will become jealous of you if they suspect you are more powerful, richer, or more accomplished than they are. They don't use charm to manage people; instead, they tend to seek pity and present themselves as victims to get you to do their bidding.

Covert narcissists are aware of social laws, display a high level of social conformity, and engage in upward social comparison. When confronted with enmity, covert narcissists don't display their aggressive self in public, because they're aware of social norms. However, they will unleash their aggression in private.

Covert narcissists are masters of sarcasm and backhanded compliments, and despise dominant hierarchies.

Dominant hierarchies remind them of where they are on the totem pole. You will find them in middle management positions that give them enough power to inflict pain on others. They also tend to be neurotic. They are obsessive and often depressed. They are shy and soft-spoken and sometimes very disagreeable.

You can identify three levels of covert narcissism:

Hypersensitive Introvert

You see these narcissists as introverted and shy, as people who tend to have a negative outlook on things. They are sensitive to criticism and may often feel that others outshine them. They may experience self-loathing and self-inadequacy and even display signs of hatred of others.

The Envious Scapegoater

At this level, narcissists have lost the ability to better their own lives and tend to play the blame game. They begin to see themselves as outcasts or as long-suffering victims, which leads to feelings of intense hostility further fueled by their lower social status. They are also tricky and sinister and use covert aggression and manipulation to punish their scapegoats. Narcissists at this level don't often have the guts to confront the people they feel have wronged them; instead, they will find a scapegoat to use as an outlet for their bottled-up rage. They use this scapegoat to regulate their moods when things don't go well.

If you're a victim of these people, you will experience sadistic punishment. They will blame you for the consequences of their self-defeating and masochistic behaviors. They misuse their powers to demean, malign, confuse, and frustrate their scapegoats.

The Punitive Avenger

At this level, narcissists have moved from merely lashing out at scapegoats to destroying perceived enemies. This is where they descend into a dangerous and deranged level, driven by a mixture of psychopathy,

Machiavellianism, and narcissism. Their victim complex becomes delusional and takes on the role of judge, jury, and executioner.

They begin to show a strong and active desire to punish people. You may observe them in seclusion, isolation, or engaging in some sort of revenge fantasy. Crisis at this level is dangerous. A loss of a job or relationship can cause them to initiate a catastrophic event. They may engage in murder, mass murder, or a shooting.

If you're a victim of a covert narcissist who is passing through these levels, you will see a progression from introversion, neuroticism, and a sense of worthlessness to a desire to punish or frustrate those they perceive as being in their way. You will also notice that they always want to make a scapegoat out of everything. In the end, they become masters at scapegoating individuals.

1.4 Narcissistic Strategies of Manipulation

All narcissists crave control - no matter where they fall on the spectrum. Which control method they decide to use depends on the type of narcissist they are. The most destructive control methods they use are the ones that make the victims question their own sanity. Covert narcissists usually employ passive-aggressive behaviors to control their victims.

The silent treatment is a form of indirect invalidation. Narcissists pretend not to hear you or walk away mid-conversation, especially when you are talking about something very important to you. Once they know that you want their attention, they avoid giving you feedback, and withhold their approval. By not responding, narcissists believe that they are punishing you. They want you to think that you are not worthy of their attention, or that you are insignificant. The more upset you become about their not validating your reality and disengaging from the conversation, the more they feel powerful. They reinforce their grandiosity by proving how easily they can control you.

Other **passive-aggressive methods** include dominating attitudes and body language that communicates contempt. Narcissists may try to dominate you with their intense cold stare.

Many people can't get over these passive-aggressive behaviors because they need some form of closure. They want to know why the narcissist is giving them the silent treatment; they don't know what they are doing wrong and want answers. The truth is, it's the narcissist's nature to use invalidation and withdrawal to nourish their feeling of grandiosity. Usually, this has very little to do with your actions, and no matter how much you try to find closure, you will most likely not get it.

Narcissists are masters of manipulation, and some of them are very good at **playing the victim**. They tell you sob stories, failures, misfortunes, exaggerate the suffering they experienced, and manipulate your empathy so that you can remain their savior and rescuer forever. They trap the victim in their web of manipulation by playing on the victim's empathy. In the long run, you will experience situations that seem like a test of your loyalty. You might end up spending a considerable part of your life validating how unique and special the narcissist is. Their superiority complex leverages your empathy as a person.

The narcissist will never be satisfied with your effort, no matter how hard you try to prove your loyalty. They compare you to others and withhold the acknowledgment of all the help you have rendered in past times. In the end, this will make you feel that you're not good enough. Playing the victim is a very effective method of control.

Mockery, public humiliation, and criticism are tools that the narcissist uses to establish control. A snide remark here about your appearance, a comment there about how silly you are, are examples of indirect tools the narcissist uses for personal gain.

If you confront them about their behavior in a public setting, they may say things like, *"Oh, it was just a joke,"* *"Don't be so sentimental,"* *"You're just overreacting,"* or *"It's just for your own good, the truth is bitter."* By doing so, they appear respectable, and if the people present laugh, the narcissist feels a boost of grandiosity in seeing your discomfort. Narcissists get their ego boost from tormenting, taunting, and punishing whoever is their chosen target. They gain control by getting an emotional reaction from others.

They create dramas and fabricate stories. Just to provoke an emotional reaction, they may even recreate history. They look for your exposed emotional buttons so they can press them and thus assure themselves of how easily they can control you. In fact, your reactions validate the narcissist's power and dominance, boosting once again their grandiosity.

Narcissists also want to control your level of self-confidence and self-worth. If you speak up for yourself, reacting to their behavior, they project their aggression onto you. They say that you're aggressive when instead you're just trying to be assertive and get your message across. So, narcissists establish control by using power struggles, games, and other subtle methods.

Narcissists are also good at **using fear as an instrument of torture and control.** They use warnings and forecasts, claiming how bad things are and predicting how your actions will only cause you pain in the long run. The reason for this behavior is very simple: believing their horrific predictions can make you more easily manipulated.

In fact, if you are fearful, you see them as your only source of wisdom, hope, and security, allowing them to have full control over you. They plant seeds of doubt and watch you questioning your own sanity. Once again, they get a boost of grandiosity by witnessing how their warnings can influence your decisions. They prove to themselves how powerful they are in your life by intimidating you into making a choice that suits them.

Narcissists do whatever it takes to **sabotage your success** because this is evidence of their power over you. They want you to turn only to them and see them as an authority on everything in your life. The more dependent you are on them, the more they can control you.

Showing an emotional reaction to a narcissist's apprehensive rage opens you up to their control since your emotions are a key thing they prey on. Your reactions demonstrate their superiority and affirm your inferiority. Therefore, be mindful of your emotional reactions. Learn discernment and how to manage your emotional state. It may take some practice, but it can be done, and it's a skill worth mastering that will benefit all areas of your life.

Some narcissists **thrive on secrecy.** Narcissists intentionally confuse you by implying that privacy and secrecy are the same. But they are not. Secrecy is used to hide something, while privacy is used to protect something. Narcissists might imply they are protecting you from something for your own good, when in fact they are hiding something that would devastate the illusion of power they have created. It could be addictions, history of abuse and violence, financial status, issues with the law, marital status - basically anything.

They also use secrecy to remain mysterious and evasive, which can be alluring to the unsuspecting person. Secrecy involves turning a blind eye to wrongdoing. It is not unusual for a narcissist to tell their victims to prove their loyalty by turning a blind eye to abuse or some kind of injustice. In this way, narcissists use secrecy to preserve control. Since they lack empathy, they don't care about the burden that they put on you. In fact, by keeping their secrets, you participate in some sort of wrongdoing just to prove your loyalty to them.

It is important to note that secrecy is not a component of any truly healthy relationship. Narcissists also expect you to keep their episodes of rage a secret, and therefore they terrify you into secrecy, even if you so much as utter a word to another party. When narcissists expect you to keep a secret, they expect you to participate in a lie and in their game of manipulation.

Gaslighting is a form of psychological manipulation where perpetrators seek to sow seeds of doubt in an individual they have targeted. The aim is to make their target question their memory, perception, and sanity. Narcissists attempt to psychologically destabilize their victims and seek to invalidate the legitimacy of the victims' experience of their own reality. Gaslighting is a form of psychological bullying. Other words that are associated with gaslighting are brainwashing and crazy-making.

You can identify gaslighting narcissists when they accuse you of issues that they themselves have. They may spread misinformation about you and start a smear campaign to ruin your reputation. If you don't have a firm grip on facts and rock-solid self-esteem, this tactic may destabilize your sanity. Gaslighting narcissists may propagate insecurity; they may fill your mind with all manner of stories that will undermine your self-confidence and sow seeds of doubt that will erode your self-worth. Once this sense of uncertainty is propagated, you become easier to manipulate.

Propaganda is also an effective tool for gaslighters. They make you believe that their perspective is the only way to view a situation. This perspective might contain half-baked facts, exaggerated ideas, rumors, and unverified allegations. In this way, they indoctrinate you and coerce you to mistrust your inner authority while surrendering your free will. Gaslighting is a method of mind control that creates a dependency on someone or something as an authority. It's a strategized effort at manipulating another person's beliefs, attitudes, or actions.

Gaslighting can include not telling the whole truth, making generalizations, insisting only on one version of events, conveniently taking things out of context, changing the facts about conversations you have had, or omitting certain details. Narcissists do this to discredit you and make sure that you feel crazy and look crazy to others. Relationships with these people will make you question your sanity.

The gaslighter is very effective in the use of **isolation**. If you try to involve external help in the relationship to make sense of difficult situations, they shoot this down and discredit these external influences. For instance, if you say you want to see a therapist for your problems, they will most likely tell you that the therapist is unqualified. Alternatively, they may use that as an opportunity to validate their claims about your insanity. Gaslighting narcissists may say something like this: *"See, that's why you see a shrink; you can't think for yourself."* This shows another method of gaslighting known as the **double bind**, which will be discussed later in the book.

Narcissists are experts at **projecting all their faults onto their victims**. For instance, if they cheat, they accuse their partner of snooping around their business and not trusting them. It's called narcissistic projection, where the narcissist uses guilt and shame to cover up their own shortcomings. This ensures that they keep control of the dynamics of the relationship and assure their dominance. Projection is a self-defense mechanism. Often, narcissists project the emotional rejections they suffered in their childhood onto their children. They may say something like, *"You are just like my father."*

It is important to say that having a difficult childhood isn't enough to justify or excuse someone when they abuse others. Many people experienced a horrific childhood but yet choose never to behave the way their abusers did. Since narcissists don't own up to their faults, it is relatively easy for them to see flaws in others and use these flaws to guilt trip them or make them do their bidding.

Through projective identification, narcissists can effectively control their victims. For instance, if you are repeatedly told that you're jealous, anxious, and have deep-seated anger issues, after a while, you may start exhibiting these behaviors. Narcissists may have a hard time understanding projection, depending on where on the spectrum they fall. Their strategies are based on them convincing the world that they are victims. They cannot be reasoned with whenever they are in these throes of aggressive projection.

Another strategy employed by narcissists is **confusing conversations.** Since they always feel the need to dominate, narcissists cause so much confusion in a discussion that the only viewpoint left will be theirs.

One of the core strategies the narcissist uses is **invalidation.** When you acknowledge someone's point of view, you validate them. You don't necessarily have to agree with them, but it means that you welcome diverse viewpoints. Narcissists never validate. For example, they may bring something unrelated into conversations that will get other people's minds stuck - hereby taking the problem off their shoulders.

Narcissists are also adept at what is called ***"hurt and rescue situations".*** They hurt their victims but still rescue them by coming up with solutions that will be only on their terms. As a result, the victim is left feeling defeated. Narcissists may even offer to take you to therapy for the anxiety they have diagnosed you with. The goal is to make you think there is something wrong with you. They deliberately cool down their rage in heated conversations to make the victim look like the aggressive one.

By the end of the conversation, the victim is emotionally overwhelmed while they remain calm.

Narcissists also use the victim's emotional state as a tool of oppression. Using invalidation, blame-shifting, projection, and gaslighting consistently, the victim is guaranteed to be in a state of emotional chaos. By the end of a conversation, the victim is completely overwhelmed and exasperated, and that's when narcissists move in for the kill. They attempt to point out that the victim's reactions and emotional state are the reason for the problems. It's a classic masterstroke of manipulation. At this point, victims start to feel that maybe they are the source of the problem.

1.5 Pathological Narcissists as Parents

When pathological narcissists become parents, they will deploy all these patterns of behavior in the relationship with their son or daughter. We can identify two main types of narcissistic parents.

The first one is the **engulfing narcissist**. This type of parent is obsessed with the child, seeing children as an extension of themselves. They have no boundaries. You might have heard of the idea that someone hasn't yet *"cut the apron strings."* This saying applies to the children of this kind of narcissistic parent. They may appear close to the child - but not emotionally. Physically they cannot stay out of their kids' lives. On the surface, everything may seem great, and there's all this attention, but the child doesn't feel like an individual, only like they are just part of the parent.

Children cannot express their wishes or feelings; the parent makes all their decisions. As they grow up, they seek a great deal of independence and are constantly tired of bringing their parents along for everything. Children struggle with getting the independence that should be a natural part of adult development.

Engulfing parents need that closeness; they need their children to provide them with emotional support. This can create a co-dependency that can be incredibly damaging to a child's development.

Engulfing narcissistic parents want to be involved in every single aspect of their children's lives. They may over-involve themselves in their kids' school activities. But they may, from time to time, undermine their children to maintain control over them. If children want to spread their wings, be independent or normal, then narcissistic parents lay down guilt trippers like *"after all I've done for you!"* to control them.

The second type of narcissistic parent is the **ignoring narcissist**. These parents don't care about the kid. They are neglectful and are only interested in what the kid can supply them. In this case, the child feels rejected, abandoned, and shows signs of incredibly low self-esteem. These children are often anxious because they don't know where comfort is coming from - or if it will come at all.

They often experience a lot of traumas because, many times, the people they are left with to supervise them can do whatever they want with them. These temporary caregivers feel so entitled because they see that the parents don't care much for the children.

The only time the child gets attention is when the narcissist is angry, and so the child learns that anger is the only real emotion. The child doesn't understand much of the parents' other feelings. This lack of emotional understanding can lead to problems later in life when the adult child tries to interact with other people but cannot do so efficiently, as no one taught them how to do that.

1.6 Signs of Narcissistic Parenting

Narcissists can inflict pain on people and still get a good night's rest because they can't empathize with other people's pain. The reason they inflict pain on people is something called narcissistic supply: narcissists always have to feed their ego. Narcissistic personality disorder could be rooted in childhood abuse. Narcissists have grown up without developing a personality. Instead of a true self, they have multiple fragmented psychic functions that work together only if they receive emotional energy from the outside.

For this reason, narcissists consider others as an extension of themselves. Without the relationship with the victim, their psyche disintegrates. So, they create a web of tormented relationships and intrigues that they need to survive, causing emotional reactions in their victims.

Narcissistic supply can be either positive or negative. The positive narcissistic supply boosts narcissists' grandiosity directly. For example, attention and admiration are positive supplies. Narcissists get a negative supply when they put down others to feel powerful, which occurs when they see their victim's emotional reactions to their abuse.

Narcissists lack empathy and may not display validation of love to their children. So, if you are an adult child of a narcissistic parent, then you have been deprived and starved of love. Most likely, you suffered emotional abuse. Your narcissistic parent withheld his love, and then he played games with you or tormented you to get some narcissistic supply from your reactions. Usually, children are not aware of the psychological and emotional abuse they suffer, and they realize it only in adulthood. Many adult children have not yet understood that their parent is a pathological narcissist. You can recognize narcissistic parenting from the following signs:

1. The mask.

Everyone is self-cautious and cares to a certain degree about what other people think about them; that's human nature. But narcissistic parents act differently at home than when they're out in public. They take pride in flaunting their social status, physical appearance, material possessions, and accomplishments. But when they no longer have an audience, they stop with the nice act. They either criticize other people or talk about them behind their back.

2. Narcissistic guilt trip.

Narcissistic parents act like they're doing you a favor by feeding, clothing, and giving you a home. Whenever they want something from you, and you say no because you have the right to say no, they remind you of how much they gave up to raise you or how much they have sacrificed for you. For example, they say, *"If I didn't have you, my life would be better."* It's a form of emotional abuse, so it's a red flag of narcissistic personality disorder.

3. Conditional love.

Healthy parents love their children no matter what. When their children do something wrong, they punish them, but it's still obvious to the children that they are loved. Narcissists don't display love for their children. They don't have the ability to love their children, so they only give out conditional love, like when you are succeeding in something or when they can brag about you to their friends. That's when they show you love and affection. But the minute you do something that embarrasses them, or if you rebel against them, they cut off your supply of love altogether. They give you the silent treatment and might even do underhanded things to get back at you. If a parent like this raises you, it's easy to see why you turn into a classic people-pleaser when you become an adult. You grow up thinking that all love is conditional because that's what your parents taught you, and so you always feel like you should prove your worth to be loved.

You constantly feel like you have to make everyone happy in order to earn love. The sense of shame is always there inside you, making you feel like you're not good enough.

4. No boundaries.

Narcissists see their children not as individuals but as extensions of themselves, so they see their children as their property. They don't see their child as a thinking human being that deserves privacy and respect. So, a narcissistic parent will always cross your boundaries, and that includes buzzing into your room without knocking, not respecting your privacy in the bathroom, and so forth.

One common and disturbing situation with girls who are raised by narcissistic mothers is the issue of a virginity check. You can imagine what goes on in the mind of a teenage girl when her mother forces her to take a virginity test in order to prove her sexual inactivity. It's traumatizing, but narcissists don't care because they see it as, "*You are mine, that's my body, that's my virginity; you're an extension of me, so I can do whatever I want to you.*" This can be quite damaging.

Narcissistic fathers decide which extracurricular activities or classes their children must take and set unrealistic expectations without considering what children have to say first. When children do stand up for themselves, narcissistic parents get easily hurt and use excuses like, *"I'm just doing what's best for you."*

5. Jealousy.

When mothers look at their daughters, they see youth and beauty. A normal mother wants to nurture that and help that flourish and grow. But a narcissistic mother is jealous and actively tries to destroy her daughter's self-esteem, even competing with her. Narcissistic mothers compete with their kids from the minute they are born. If someone pays more attention to the child than to her, then she resents the child.

Narcissistic fathers may become extremely jealous when children start seeking independence. The father wants to be the alpha-male, and he is in competition with his son as soon as he grows up. When the daughter has romantic relationships, her partners are never good enough for the narcissistic father.

6. Control.

Narcissistic parents protect their egos, and if they feel they are losing control or their egos are hurt, they become cruel, blaming, and offensive. A healthy parent controls their children for good, but a narcissistic parent wants to decide everything: your career, who you can date, and when you can move out. When you start thinking for yourself and stop asking for their validation, they start bullying you.

7. Taking credit for your accomplishments.

Narcissistic parents usually do this in public but not in private.

8. Lack of empathy.

Narcissistic parents cannot feel other people's pain and, even worse, often get a kick out of other people's misery (negative narcissistic supply). So, if you've ever been in a situation where you just needed your parents to empathize with you and tell you *"Everything's going to be okay,"* and they genuinely cannot do that, it might be a sign that they have a narcissistic personality disorder. Possibly worse is the fact that they may even appear to enjoy your pain. It's weird for a parent to do that, and that's why narcissism is a personality disorder.

9. Infantilization.

Narcissistic parents do their best to keep their children in a child-like dependent state. They don't want their children to grow up and gain independence. They can't let that happen: how could they then fill their supply from their children? For this reason, they try to keep their children around for as long as possible by training them to be helpless. They don't teach their kids how to cook or the other basic things you're supposed to teach your child.

As a result, the child always feels like, *"I'm dependent on my parents, and I can't make it without them."* In this way, narcissistic parents are engaging in psychological abuse because they constantly put their children down while reminding them that they're helpless. You never even try to reach out for help; you always feel like you have to come back to your parents because your self-esteem is low and weak. You feel like the whole world is against you. But the truth is that there are people out there who would be happy to help you and love you more than your parents could. Narcissistic parents don't want you to know that, because if you leave them, then they lose their source of supply.

10. Never admitting wrong.

Never expect a narcissist to apologize. They won't because they don't feel bad about what they have done. Sometimes they acknowledge something, and then later, they'll tell you that it didn't happen. If they're not gaslighting you, they're probably turning things around to make themselves the victims. They never admit their wrongs.

11. Projecting bad traits onto you.

Your parents could be visibly selfish, inconsiderate, evil, and negative. But for some odd reason, they throw those things onto you as if you are the one with these traits.

12. Destroying your self-esteem.

A narcissistic parent can openly call you a fat slob, but some do it more subtly, like, *"Oh, are you going to wear that shirt outside? It's a little bit small around your waist."* This is underhanded and passive-aggressive but subtle enough to plant small seeds of insecurity in your head. These seeds germinate and push your self-esteem into the ground. As a result, you grow up having no self-love, no confidence, and you can't stop paying attention to that voice in your head that says you're not worthy or good enough.

Another way in which they lower your self-esteem is by comparing you to other people. They compare you to other kids, making it seem like they got the short end of the stick by having you: *"Why couldn't I have a child who acts like this or acts like that?"* Even if you did the best you could, it would never be good enough for them because they always find a person to compare you to. They just have to make you feel bad about yourself because they have a wound within themselves.

They have shame within themselves, and so to suppress it, they try to throw that shame on you.

11. They play the victim and never take responsibility.

Even if your argument is reasonable or logical, narcissistic parents manipulate you and point fingers. They never take responsibility for their actions and marginalize your needs and feelings. They play mind games with you, but they get off easy because they play their victim card well.

13. Causing drama.

Narcissistic parents enjoy drama because they feed off emotional responses. For example, if you have siblings, your narcissistic parent will try to make you not like each other. Moreover, narcissistic parents tend to have a favorite called "the golden child" to get a positive narcissistic supply and a "scapegoat child" to get a negative supply.

Narcissistic parents make scapegoats feel like trash - like these children don't matter and are inadequate - and put golden children on a pedestal. But remember, they don't really love the golden child; they just love the image that the golden child represents. They try to pit siblings against each other, and since they live for drama, they thrive in situations with the potential for highly explosive emotional reactions.

They may sit you down to talk about your problems and make it seem like they're trying to get in your head to help you, but they're actually trying to get an emotional response out of you and make you upset. You will probably leave in tears a conversation that started with just a question. Often, they need to call family meetings because they are running low on drama and are searching for an emotional response.

1.7 Enablers

Enablers are the people who support and defend the narcissist. Narcissists recruit enablers to their side. Enablers are usually called "flying monkeys," and they enable the narcissist by tolerating their behavior or saving them from the catastrophes they create in their lives.

These are the people who say, *"She's your mother; you need to forgive her"* or *"He's your father; you need to forgive him."* Enablers usually don't have a malicious motive and often think they're helping - but they are not. They reinforce the narcissist's behavior and thus make the problem worse. Nothing is happening to prevent the narcissist from having their way, however. Narcissists are still receiving the attention that they seek. There are no consequences to their behaviors. This enables the narcissist, whether people choose to believe that or not.

Every time an enabler draws a line in the sand, the narcissist crosses it - and the enabler just keeps on drawing more lines. Eventually, narcissists are going to realize that these lines mean nothing. The only reason enablers put up with abusive behavior is that they have been conditioned to believe that it's okay and there is no alternative but to continue the relationship with a toxic and abusive person.

Enablers believe they're proving something to the narcissist by staying in the relationship. Well, they are proving that narcissists can treat them however they want, and they'll put up with it because the narcissist's well-being matters to them more than their own. Enablers tell the narcissists that they don't have to treat them any better because they don't believe they deserve better treatment.

That's unhealthy and toxic; it's also exactly what narcissists want.

They want you to set yourself on fire to keep them warm, and nothing you do for them will ever be enough. Narcissists take emotional supply from other people by abusing them, and enablers teach the narcissist that this behavior is okay. More than that, they're teaching it to themselves.

There's a large amount of guilt involved in relationships with narcissists. These relationships are like those with infants; they are completely one-sided. Infants need no reciprocation, and narcissists stay in that infantilized emotional state forever, needing and taking without seeing other people as people at all. It is where boundaries come in. Boundaries are the lines in the sand that we draw: *"If you cross this line, I will leave."* Boundaries can work with narcissists if you enforce consequences because they know the difference between right and wrong.

Enablers don't have clear boundaries and don't pose a threat when the narcissist crosses a boundary. This teaches the narcissist that the boundaries don't mean anything, and consequently, they don't have to respect them. People treat us the way we allow them to treat us. Therefore, enablers should respect themselves, protect themselves, and stop enabling the disorder that is controlling and ruining everyone's life. No contact is the best strategy for dealing with narcissists and their enablers. A narcissist cannot exist alone, so there are always enablers. When these enablers are identified, they should be subject to the same rules as the narcissist because they are damaging you as well.

The Enabling Father

Narcissists can be very clever and cunning when choosing a mate. They look for somebody weaker than them, a person who abides by their rules. They look for someone they can manipulate, somebody who overlooks the abuse they do to others, somebody they can control.

The narcissist can change the way someone else thinks, and if others don't think for themselves, they become enablers. Enablers allow the narcissist to do dirty deeds. They keep their mouths shut even when they know full well that the narcissist is doing something horrible and even abusive.

Once the narcissistic mother controls all relationships between family members, she sees the enabler as yet another plaything. She creates a divide between the siblings and the enabling father. Usually, he is frightened of something. He is afraid that he will lose money, lose the social status that the narcissist provides, won't be cared for, and that his narcissistic wife will turn on him, making him a victim. The enabler sits by and allows his children to be abused; he is too frightened and will do anything that the narcissist demands. He turns his back on his children, even though they are being abused physically, emotionally, or sexually. He neglects his children entirely.

The narcissistic family may seem normal from the outside, and this appearance is a protection for the narcissistic mother who doesn't want to get caught abusing her victims. Nobody would believe children when they speak about their parent's cruelty. There is a denial system between the family members around the narcissist. There is the implicit agreement that the narcissist is entitled to act cruelly and should bear no responsibility for hurting others. As the second-highest authority in the house, the enabling parent endorses the narcissist, creating a huge problem. The father has no excuses for his behavior; he could have done something about it but refused to do so. After brainwashing, the enabler agrees with the narcissist's lies; he encourages his children's lack of communication because that keeps the narcissist off his back and happy. These parents take no responsibility for themselves nor their actions.

If the child feels abused, then it's the child's fault for being "*overly sensitive.*"

The Enabling Mother

A malignant narcissist could not abuse their children without the endorsement of the other parent. The enabling mother's life goal is to make the narcissist happy. She is not aware of the narcissistic manipulation that makes her feel insecure, tormented, and constantly inadequate in making the narcissist happy. The narcissist strategically uses the enabler's need to please. A child born by a narcissistic father and an enabling mother will be inevitably abused. The enabling mother doesn't consider the children's needs but only sees the narcissist's unhappiness, and she wants to make her narcissistic partner happy. The enabling mother may gang up with the narcissistic father against the child.

She may seem distracted or uninvolved while the narcissist abuses the child. She may even find a way to be out of the house when it happens. The narcissistic family may seem normal from the outside, and this appearance is a protection for the narcissistic father who doesn't want to get caught abusing his victims. Nobody would believe children when they speak about their parent's cruelty. There is a denial system among the family members around the narcissist. There is the implicit agreement that the narcissist is entitled to act cruelly and should bear no responsibility for hurting others. As the second-highest authority in the house, the enabling parent endorses the narcissist, creating a huge problem. The narcissistic and enabling parents can have such strong faith in this lie that they feel no dissonance. The narcissistic father abuses the scapegoat child because he claims he deserves it, and the enabling mother agrees.

PART TWO
NARCISSISTIC MOTHERS

LET'S START BY TALKING about how difficult it is to view a mother as a source of something negative. Regardless of the religion you practice or the culture you grew up in, the mother is worshiped everywhere in the world. And this is a beautiful thing! But we must also be cautious because this same mother worship protects bad mothers and allows transgenerational traumas to linger on and on.

The "taboo" of speaking badly about mothers makes it more difficult for people who have been affected by narcissistic mothers to seek healing. Adult children of narcissistic parents are often plagued with so much guilt and a sense of deep obligation and shame that they feel duty-bound to keep whatever happens in the family secret, even when it is shredding their lives.

Unfortunately, trauma and these kinds of negative emotions can (and if left unchecked will) rob us of the joy of life. They thrive when we don't talk about them or when we don't make enough room for them to dissipate.

The issue of toxic mothers challenges the status quo in so many ways but does need to be addressed. The main problem with experiencing narcissism from a mother is that you often feel unloved and unacknowledged. It's difficult to share your experience because narcissists, especially narcissistic mothers, can be very good at creating the perfect image of their family for outsiders. The idea of something bad going on inside the family can seem almost unbelievable to an outsider, especially when it comes from a child.

As children, it's already difficult to get validation and acknowledgment. In fact, children often don't have the competence or the ability to understand what's going on and to state their needs in a way that makes other people receptive and respectful of their young voices. Additionally, the narcissistic mother can create a tough barrier to penetrate. And in many cases, it just gets worse and worse over time.

There are so many men and women who are suffering in silence. Even in the last years of life, their mothers are still tormenting them with guilt. Even when they're on their deathbed, these mothers are still emotionally treating their adult children like doormats and keep acting horribly.

It is important to state that when you grow up in a narcissistic family, some toxic dynamics, which aren't immediately apparent, create many invisible wounds. This kind of hidden abuse is the most painful scenario and leaves the most Complex Post-Traumatic Stress Disorder (CPTSD) residue. It's so difficult to live with these invisible wounds because you can't quite pinpoint what happened.

These hidden wounds can result from a series of small but repetitive traumatic events that have silenced you and made you feel continually worthless as if there's something wrong with you and you are somehow damaged. This is the message you receive from growing up in dysfunctional families driven by a narcissistic parent.

You get to the point where you can't even think for yourself because you are over-reliant on the opinion of others. You are just suffering in silence and sometimes don't even admit this to yourself. The healing journey from this situation will be long and difficult, and often impossible without the help of a psychotherapist.

Your narcissistic mother most likely will never be officially diagnosed. Still, you eventually recognize her for the crazy-making trail she leaves behind. For example, she plays mind games to covertly provoke conflict between family members, even putting her children against each other. Narcissistic mothers are extremely damaging and cause their children much pain.

When a narcissistic mother has children, she doesn't have them for the same reason a healthy mother does. She has them for the sole purpose of satisfying her unmet needs. Often, narcissistic mothers consider their children real-life extensions of themselves. They are unable to unconditionally love their children since they expect something from them in return.

2.1 The Narcissistic Mother and the Roles She Chooses for Her Children

A narcissistic mother assigns different roles to her children, and this has a tremendous effect on them. She typically puts her children in three major roles: the golden child, the scapegoat, and the invisible or lost child.

The **scapegoat** is the child who is *"never good enough"*. No matter what these children do, they never satisfy the narcissistic mother, who always finds ways to make them feel like they have never achieved anything. If children ever express any anger or resentment toward the mother, then she punishes them severely.

The **golden child** is a representation of the grandiose self of the mother. The mother might focus all her attention on this child, and sometimes the dysfunctional relationship with the "golden son" can even be deeper than the relationship she has with her husband. The golden child is the opposite of the scapegoat child. The golden child can never do any wrong; the narcissistic mother idolizes them. She always pays a lot of attention to any tiny accomplishment that this child achieves.

The invisible or **lost child** is the most neglected. The narcissistic mother is not very interested in this child. She forgets to do certain things with this child or doesn't want to consider this child's needs. She may even forget that the lost child has the same needs as other children.

Let's analyze these situations one by one. Labeling these familial roles can help us gain a broader perspective. Adult children of narcissistic mothers should not adopt these labels permanently, identifying themselves with their role. But we can use this classification to recognize something that we were not conscious of. Understanding allows us to disengage from the blame game.

The Golden Child

The narcissistic mother worships the golden child. This child reflects everything she wants for herself, particularly in the area of an emotional relationship. Therefore, her view of her child is what we would call a perverted view. It's an unhealthy view and is derived from the fact that the mother has a tremendous void in her own life.

The narcissistic mother looks at her golden child as a trophy while consistently reinforcing that her child is perfect, superior, and charming. There's nothing too good for them, and that idea is instilled in golden children at a very young age. So, they do not get the things they need: love, validation, attention, protection, support, affirmation, and correction where necessary.

Narcissistic mothers make their golden children feel superior to everybody else, and as a consequence, these children grow up to potentially become narcissists or at least to have narcissistic traits. It's important to know that everything the narcissistic mother does is about her; it's not about her child. The child is being used as a tool, and again this manipulation comes with a price.

Golden children are never able to grow emotionally outside their mothers' control. Their confidence, self-respect, and identity are tied to their mothers' approval. Everything they do, even their relationship with their spouse when they get married, is based on their mothers' needs. Of course, they also experience difficulty connecting emotionally with people in a healthy way.

The golden child of a narcissistic mother is often a son and the last kid of the family, but not always. Golden sons and golden daughters are not enmeshed with their narcissistic mothers in the same way because the Oedipus complex and the emotional incest happen only between mother and son. There is always a fusion of identities, but the daughter's fusion has more projective contents than the son's fusion. For this reason, generally speaking, adult golden sons are more likely to have NPD than golden daughters.

When the narcissistic mother looks at her golden son, she sees him through a perverted lens. She looks at her son in an unhealthy way. She looks up to him to fulfill her emotional emptiness and provide the attention she craves. She also turns to her son to validate and support her emotionally.

The narcissistic mother desires a husband she can look up to, someone she expects to fulfill her dreams and expectations. Most of the time, her man is incapable of this, so the narcissistic mother turns to her son to make this happen. The golden son then becomes meshed with his mother emotionally. He's getting many toxic emotions from his mother, who is looking to him to fill her needs. Therefore, the mother begins to see him as her trophy. He can do nothing wrong.

A narcissist's biggest fear is their supply being cut off. To counter this, a narcissistic mother deploys psychological warfare strategies against the golden son at an early age. The main strategy is called **emotional incest**. We're talking about seduction: the mother seduces the golden son to replace the male figure in her life. The mother sees the golden son as a replacement for her neglectful father or for her husband. The mother emotionally marries the golden son, and he is expected to meet her emotional needs. If she's married, she emasculates her husband

and chooses the golden son as an emotional replacement.

While, for the most part, the relationship with her son isn't sexual, it is nonetheless perverse, meaning that it is not the normal way a mother should relate with her children. Therefore, sometimes you can see a mother with her golden son at a young age (even into the teen years) flirting with him and touching him inappropriately. That may not be strictly sexual, but it is very inappropriate, especially if that son has gone through puberty and into adolescence. As the son grows intellectually and physically, his emotions are arrested, and he always feels like he needs to satisfy the mother's wishes and demands.

If the golden child tries to pull back and be independent, that decision is met with the mother's vengeance. She may employ a lot of different tactics, including drama, manipulation, control, and lies. This vengeance brings hell into the children's life because they are looking to emancipate themselves, and the narcissistic mother has a serious problem with that, even to the point where she sabotages the child's independence, dreams, and visions.

The Scapegoat

The scapegoat child gets the blame for the family's problems. The family's burdens and responsibilities are usually placed on this child. If this were you, you might have had the courage to speak out but were bullied, threatened, and dominated back into submission. There are a lot of unspoken rules in narcissistic families, and emotional pain is hidden. There's an undercurrent of competition and sibling rivalry, and it seems like children constantly need to fight for their parent's love and attention. Narcissistic parents feel threatened by scapegoats because they are the only ones with enough strength and courage to expose family members for who they are. The scapegoat is very sensitive and aware of the truth about what's going on behind the impression of the family that the narcissistic parent is trying to display. If you are the scapegoat, or the black sheep, you may feel like nothing is ever good enough.

Your narcissistic mother may be happy with you one day and bitterly disappointed the next. If you speak out about how you feel, saying that perhaps you've been treated unjustly, then your narcissistic mother is quick to put you in your place. She relies on unpredictable mood swings and bullying tactics when dealing with the scapegoat because she avoids taking responsibility for her unfair treatment of her children. You may have always been the one to blame for everything that goes wrong; you may have been picked on and repeatedly put down.

Narcissistic mothers take credit for everything that goes right, but it's the scapegoat's fault for anything that goes wrong within the family.

This dysfunctional parenting style creates a separation between the children because the mother chooses one of them to be the negative example in the family. Since your narcissistic mother has set this dynamic up, she often fails to protect you when other family members taunt and verbally brutalize you. So, everything plays out exactly as she expects.

The scapegoat is a role narcissistic mothers assign to the most outspoken, extremely intuitive children who are the first to notice a problem. Since scapegoats are the whistleblowers, they are often accused of being liars, mentally ill, or exaggerating. Of course, outsiders who aren't aware of the narcissistic parent's tactics to control the family will believe in that. Therefore, scapegoats often feel rejected, isolated, and alone, as if they don't belong anywhere.

The scapegoat experiences their childhood feeling burdened with all the faults, wrongdoings, and neglect of the narcissistic parent. If you are the scapegoat, no matter how many A-plus grades you get on your school report or whether you win a trophy or are recognized for your excellent achievements, you are minimized, unacknowledged, or completely ignored by the narcissistic mother.

You will never meet your mother's expectations. It is impossible to meet her standards, and of course, you will never be as good as her favorite and chosen golden child. Scapegoats often carry from their childhood into adulthood all the heavy feelings of guilt, shame, and not being good enough. If you are still in contact with your narcissistic mother, she continues to imply that you are to blame for all that's wrong in the family or in her life. You may still be the one that the narcissistic mother is most ashamed of and disappointed in.

She manipulates other family members to gang up against you by focusing on everything wrong with you. This behavior conveniently takes the focus away from the real perpetrator, who is, of course, her. It's interesting to think about the manipulation that's going on.

Once you have been labeled as the black sheep, which has been your permanent role in the family, all the other family members are entitled to feel better about themselves. They begin to believe that they are healthier and more obedient to the narcissistic mother than you, and again this creates further division within the family.

Another important point is that scapegoat children may fully internalize all their narcissistic mother's criticism and shame. For this reason, scapegoats develop this "inner scapegoating," the internal dialogue that constantly reminds them of how bad and flawed they are.

It is extremely toxic to a young impressionable child whose identity is still being formed. Adult scapegoat children may struggle with low self-esteem and often continue to feel deeply inadequate and unlovable. Therefore, they become super sensitive to any potential signs of approval or disapproval. Adult scapegoat children also tend to suppress a huge amount of abandonment anxiety because they were emotionally or even physically abandoned by their narcissistic mother over and over again.

These are all critical aspects of the profound impact that a toxic family dynamic may continue to have on adult relationships. Perhaps you may still have issues with authority. Maybe you're still used to justifying yourself or proving your worth somehow.

It's an unconscious pattern that you are perpetuating because you don't realize how powerful these dysfunctional family dynamics are.

Once you wake up and understand, you can let go of that label. You can break that pattern by choosing to think and behave completely differently. It's not easy, but a good therapist can help you. You can learn to choose your battles and not always be defensive. You don't have to feel victimized all the time. You need to become more self-aware and notice if you are still trying to get your parents' approval or validation. Maturing into adulthood means understanding that you cannot have a healthy relationship with a narcissist. You need to process your feelings of frustration, loneliness, rage, and grief.

On a positive note, the scapegoat is the truth-teller. They are the ones who are unable to tolerate lies and injustice. Scapegoats often show tremendous strength because they've survived a lot of criticism and shaming and are used to being threatened by the narcissist. They're accustomed to being shunned by the rest of the family.

Scapegoats refuse to stay silent and often initiate change. They are the ones most likely to escape, heal, and bring an end to this transgenerational dysfunction. If this has been your allocated role, you have lots of strengths. So, I guess you know that I wrote this book because I feel deeply inspired by scapegoats to help break these narcissistic behavioral patterns.

The Lost Child

Lost children are often quiet. They have their back up against the wall, don't cause a lot of waves, do pretty well in school, and might even be a bit artistic. Often, the lost child is so quiet that the parents say, "*Oh, that child is such a blessing; they don't cause any trouble.*"

There's no big deal, but when lost children do find themselves in trouble, it's serious trouble. Their needs are not being met on any level. It's like they're invisible and get neither blame nor praise from the narcissistic mother.

This is the child who just seemingly doesn't exist in the family. The basic needs of this kid are ignored across the board. Essentially, this child is alone and finds it hard to let anybody into their private world. There are no natural or easy connections between these children and other people because they feel very lonely and isolated.

Lost children get depressed, but they are also very independent. Since they never felt valuable during childhood, they don't feel valued as adults. As they become teenagers, they feel unlovable and undeserving of trust. They don't even think that their thoughts are worth hearing. Unfortunately, these children may fall into substance abuse, drugs, alcohol, sex addiction, eating disorders, gambling, and other addictive behaviors.

Since lost children are not used to having any sort of attention, they don't expect it and don't seek it out in their lives. These are generally not the kids who later become narcissists. However, since they become self-reliant, they sometimes have twisted ideas of what life is all about, coming out of a toxic home.

When they leave home, the family will often not even realize they're gone. At school, they might be the kid in the back of the room that nobody speaks to or thinks about. They don't join clubs or groups. These are the kids who are out back smoking. If they do get involved with others, they're involved with kids like them, the outcasts. It is dangerous and a part of the reason why they sometimes get on the wrong side of the law as they get older.

Other lost children choose to throw themselves into school, get good grades, go to the best college, do all the right things, but still never get noticed. These are the ones who are driven by the need for the approval they never got and will never get from their parents.

If you meet a lost child out in the world, they probably appear shy and introverted, but in reality, this person is not just quiet but disconnected from other people. Sadly, lost children display this isolation throughout their lives, even when they become adults and get into relationships.

They are also more likely to read a book or watch TV or play video games or do anything to avoid conflict. They often don't want to deal with others since they don't like contact. They may also be artistic or musical, and quite often, they're genuinely talented individuals. However, since they don't want to be hurt, they're always careful to avoid getting too close to anyone. If they happen to trust someone enough to get into a relationship, they become dependent and needy.

Unless lost children understand what they're dealing with and go through the healing process they need, they are in great danger of becoming addicts.

The saddest part of this whole story is that their cycle continues, so they often become the absentee parent or the parent who can't be emotionally connected to their children, which is terrible. Obesity can be an issue for the lost child, as well as anorexia, addiction to the internet or video games. They might become workaholics, but whatever it is, they're going to throw themselves into something, and we just have to hope it is something healthy - which usually it is not. The upside is that they do work well alone, are self-reliant, very often quite intelligent, and well-read. If you give them a chance and they get close enough to you, they can become great listeners.

So, how can a lost child recover? The first thing is getting into therapy to get in touch with the rage built up all over these years. There's also a significant amount of fear in lost children because they often have questions and concerns. They have things they want to talk about, and there's nobody to listen to them.

Lost children have to recognize the pain of the past. They should acknowledge their core wound and take it to the next level of healing. If you are a lost child, you should realize the emotional emptiness you have carried with you throughout your life and acknowledge that you are indeed lost. Acknowledge, recognize, and own the fact that you came out of a toxic home; don't deny it anymore.

Once you have recognized the pain and the situation, and own it for what it was, then you can face it. You can begin to form deeper relationships in your life and with yourself. You have to get to know yourself first. If you have noticed yourself playing the victim, it's time to let go of that feeling. Learn to make decisions and set long-term personal goals. As you heal, you're going to find out that you're not weird, you're not bad, and there isn't anything wrong with you. The fault was just your family and the broken person in your family that caused you to feel like the lost child.

You can start healing by changing your perception of yourself and the world around you. If you previously thought, "*If I don't get emotionally involved, I won't get hurt,*" or "*I can't make a difference anyway,*" or "*It's better not to draw attention to myself,*" change that thought pattern. Now begin thinking, "*I deserve attention,*" "*I do make a difference,*" and "*If I don't get emotionally involved, I'll never have meaningful connections.*" You can't allow yourself to be defined by a narcissist. None of us can allow ourselves to be defined by a narcissist because the narcissist looks at us through an ugly, dirty, broken lens. Every lost child on the planet must realize that nothing the narcissist told us was true about the world, and we owe it to ourselves to rediscover the world for what it really is and who we really are - then rediscover ourselves.

2.2 Types of Narcissistic Mothers

If you've dealt with a narcissistic mom, the chances are good that one of the following things happened: you were very controlled, you were ignored, or a combination of both. In any case, you were robbed of a healthy normal childhood, and very often face additional struggles as an adult.

Narcissistic mothers exist on a spectrum, and this spectrum ranges from neglectful to tyrannical. The first step of the healing journey is becoming aware of all abusive situations you might have suffered.

The Severely Overt Narcissistic Mother

This kind of mother will make you feel unloved because she is self-absorbed and always seeking attention. Life for her is a stage where she always has to be the star. Such mothers can bring up their kids, show them off to their friends and tell them, *"You see what I have produced; my kids are my pride and joy."* This can be very damaging for boys because they learn that this is the only way to be in the world. The son can't be fully himself while trying to always be the kind of man his mother expects him to be. On the other hand, when her daughter becomes a young woman, the overt narcissistic mother begins to compete with her, quickly turning nasty.

This kind of mother shows you also how much of a burden you are to her. Once again, self-absorption takes the upper hand. She tells you how much money it cost her to raise you and how much you are draining her because she never has time for herself. One day the narcissistic mother will push you out of the nest. She will want you out as soon as possible, without giving you the proper tools to grow up, go out into the world, and succeed.

Other overt narcissistic mothers are the opposite; they want to keep you with them always and forbid you to leave them because they will feel so abandoned. This kind of narcissistic mother rewards you with co-dependency. Another kind of severely overt narcissistic mother wants to feel needed, and yet at the same time, she's going to push you away when your needs become too much. She doesn't want you to be too self-reliant or independent because then there is the threat of you not meeting her needs.

The overt narcissistic mother doesn't acknowledge your emotions; there's no room for you to fully express yourself basically because the moment you take up too much space, you're threatening her. So, she always tries to tear you down, but she doesn't acknowledge when she hurts you. She says things that should never be said.

As soon as you turn into an independent teenager with your own life, you will reach a competitive level with her. Then, she will continue to tear you down to keep building herself up. This type of mother has to always be on top. She is the kind of woman who wants to be perpetually young. She tries to hang out with your friends, and she even tries to take over your peer group. She also triangulates between siblings.

Triangulation is incredibly toxic, especially in a family. Narcissistic mothers whisper one thing to one child, another thing to another child, set them against each other, create conflict, and sit back to enjoy the drama they have just created. But of course, if you try to confront her about this, she would deny everything. She's the saint. She is always blame-shifting and guilt-tripping everybody around her. She's the center of attention, and it's all about her. This is the end result of triangulation. Later in life, if you've been able to dig for the truth and figure out what really happened, you can confirm your stories with the stories of your brothers or sisters or cousins, then you will see a much more accurate picture. Of course, that picture will be tainted if the other people have become flying monkeys, meaning that they share the same distortion of reality, in which case the conflict only mounts. Unfortunately, contemporary families are often dysfunctional and divided. For this reason, being an outspoken person can cost you a lot. It may cost you banishment, which is encoded in our genes as the worst form of punishment. When you're outside of the clan, when you've been pushed away from the tribe, you can be threatened by all sorts of predators.

Loneliness can be so devastating to us because we feel threatened and exposed. You never feel heard or seen or able to succeed, so you get trapped between shame and guilt. If you don't do enough, you're going to be ashamed. If you do too much, you're going to feel guilty. Either way, your family will make you feel awful. I've heard of young daughters being very successful only to find that their success threatens their relationship with their mother.

What happens is that the mother can't enjoy her daughter's success because she is convinced that the daughter has made a choice between her and success. In this situation, if the daughter knew the person she was dealing with, it would be much easier to decide not to go back to the toxic mother. But because children dare not to separate from the idea that mothers need to be revered, the daughter is in conflict. The overt narcissistic mother gives conflicting messages, like proudly showing you off on the one hand, then subtly putting you down on the other.

The Severely Narcissistic and Sadistic Mother

These mothers lock up their kids in their rooms. They are often alcoholics and completely neglectful. They let the streets raise their children and don't care what happens to them. There is a tremendously deep level of abandonment. Sometimes there are a series of new husbands or boyfriends. These stepfathers sometimes sexually abuse these kids, creating an unhealthy environment to raise a child. So many families don't deserve to raise kids because they don't provide a safe environment. Unfortunately, the result is a very high number of people raised this way, struggling to fend for themselves. They have been shattered inside because they haven't received the sustenance, love, compassion, and protection they needed as children by virtue of being born. Adult children of this kind of narcissistic mothers always have a Complex Post Traumatic Stress Disorder (CPTSD).

The Enmeshed Mother

She is the most covert of all narcissistic mothers. Instead of teaching you to build a life of your own, she snaps on the emotional handcuffs and never lets you go. Enmeshed mothers can seem like they're just perfect, always taking care of their kids, but instead are turning their children into lifelong infants. The enmeshed mother will never allow you to grow up. If you're a man, you'll always be stuck between this half-man/half-child state.

Children in this situation are emotionally stunted in so many ways because they have been imprinted with the message that it's not safe outside of their home and that it's always better to stay with their mom. It is a form of co-dependency training that doesn't allow the children to go out there and learn the skills of survival and assertiveness to succeed. Their independence is not supported, and instead, they are punished for trying to be self-sufficient. This scenario can be extremely damaging, especially for boys, because there's a borderline component here: the fear of abandonment. Since the narcissistic mother has a bad relationship with the father of her children, she pours all her love and attention into the son, making him the center of her world. If the father isn't gone, most of the time he neglects his son as well as his wife. She then turns him into a monster in the boy's eyes, and the boy takes over the burden of the dad, who is not present. In these circumstances, the son has to grow up very quickly and be rewarded for being there for his mommy. He essentially becomes her surrogate husband.

It's something that's called *parentification*. This sometimes creates sensitive, openhearted, and giving men, but the problem is that their boundaries are very permeable. There isn't enough give-and-take in the relationship, and they just work themselves to the bone to satisfy a woman because that's what they did for their mothers. These men take that dynamic outside of the relationship with their mom and continue it in their romantic relationships.

The problem for these men is that it's easy for them to attract other narcissists, sociopaths, psychopaths, and borderline women who end up destroying them. Adult children of enmeshed narcissistic mothers, both sons and daughters, feel hurt deep inside because they are like, *"I'm doing everything I can, I'm the best version of myself, my mom raised me with the right values, and yet I keep getting my ass kicked. Why?"* Now you know why. So, the enmeshing mother may think in her mind that she's doing the right thing, but she's not; she is suffocating her children. A healthy relationship between a parent and a child has to come from respect and the giving of space. Children need to develop their own separate identity and succeed in society. Healthy parents support that independence and separation.

2.3 Narcissistic Mothers and Their Sons

A man's relationship with his mother is just as complicated as a relationship between a daughter and her mother. In order to move forward, men will have to understand what is at the root of their struggles.

A first specific area of the relationship between the male child and the narcissistic mother is her behavior with all the people who have some interactions with her son. The overt narcissistic mother is aggressive, abrasive, and intolerant. For her, everybody else is an asshole; everybody else is stupid - especially other women. So, it's a little bit easier to see that this person is narcissistic, but you could have narcissistic moms who aren't so easy to spot. A covert narcissist mother, on the other hand, may seem to actually care about her son, and you might not be able to understand that she is fostering codependency.

In both situations - overt and covert - narcissistic mothers use their sons as a source of supply. There is an investment happening; there is an unconscious desire to consume the son and create a dependency that will provide a continuous source of narcissistic supply. The son cannot go out and become a separate individual from his mother. A narcissistic mother's agenda is to make sure that she's number one, to ensure that this young man never goes out and leaves her. As a result, other women are considered a threat, just like his friends. She finds something wrong with every person that her son brings into the house. She even has a problem with his friends' parents, as well as with each of her son's teachers.

Another big trouble is the relationship with the father of her son. Often narcissistic mothers marry very co-dependent men and put them down in front of the children. Lots of men have witnessed how their narcissistic mothers have battered their fathers in front of them - perhaps not in front of the neighbors and other family members, but behind closed doors. This kind of chaos happens when you have a narcissistic mother and a co-dependent father emasculated and constantly beaten down.

If you're the son of this kind of couple, you probably have no idea how to face such dynamics. You are being abandoned emotionally by this man who has just run out of steam. He goes to work, comes home to be criticized, and has to sleep on the couch. Nothing he does is ever good enough. There's always something to complain about, and so this man, who should teach you how to stand up for yourself and not be abused, has abandoned you. On the flip side of the coin, you also identify with your father. So, every time your mom puts him down, she's doing the same thing to you.

She's trying to make sure that you feel dependent upon her and obligated to her. She's trying to find a way to make sure that you don't do what your dad has done to her, which is to abandon her. Because from her point of view, that's what your dad did. Mom needs to believe that her son has put her at the center of his life. Therefore, the son of a narcissistic mother is terrified, living in a state of survival. There's also an obstacle to the development of the self, which is also a problem in terms of emotional growth. The young boy doesn't feel free enough to explore his environment without fear. There's a lot of insecurity in the young boy who has a narcissistic mom, which carries over to adolescence when this young man wants to bring home a date.

The mom will find a problem with the date and will actually gaslight them, creating many problems. The son will get the message that the mom is not happy that he brought that person home. Statements like,

"That girl only wants you for your money," "That girl's going to go out and get pregnant by you," or *"You're going to have to support her and some kids for the rest of your life,"* will be thrown around. You could be twelve, and that's the kind of crap that your mother may tell you to make sure you get the message.

It also happens that the narcissistic mother gets sick the minute her son wants to go out to play baseball or tells her he has a girlfriend. Mommy would get sick, and the boy would have to abandon everything and prove to his mother that she is number one in his life. This dynamic gets repeated over and over. There's a lot of fear of disappointing your mom. You feel obligated to put her needs first, and when you're focusing on trying to please mom, you're losing yourself. As a consequence, you have low self-esteem and lack an identity. Besides, when you're around other people, you feel anxiety, but it's absolutely not your fault.

As you grow older, get married, and have children, your narcissistic mother becomes a bigger problem. In fact, she wants to make sure that also the women in your life and even your children understand that she comes first. A narcissistic mom sees the women in your life as competitors. Your wife will definitely feel like there's a mistress in the room, and even though you are not sleeping with your mom, this energy will be a part of your life. You will be conflicted if you're not aware that mom is a narcissist and that she's trying to control you, that she wants to take center stage and doesn't care about the chaos she's creating in your life. If you're not aware of that, you might be confused and push your wife back. On the one hand, you would like to stand by your wife, but on the other hand, you've been conditioned since childhood to worry about mommy.

You might also have a tremendous fear of cutting your wife off, which is what your mom wants you to do. If you divorce your wife, it means that your mother has exploited your primitive fear of losing her. This fear prevailed over that of losing your wife. You are in an infant-like state, and for a newborn the loss of a mother is akin to death. You might not realize that your mother is intrusive, that she speaks ill of your wife. She has no compassion or empathy for you, nor for your wife. You might not recognize that mom talks behind everybody's back. You might not recognize that mom has a difficult time maintaining friendships, has to prove herself superior to everybody, or that she has a drinking problem, a shopping problem, a gambling problem, or some other addiction that you're not aware of. Since she has primed you to fear being able to set boundaries, you may have marital problems or relationship problems with females who can't stand the intrusiveness of your mother.

This tug-of-war in the mind of the sons of narcissistic mothers can be serious. On the one hand, they love their mothers, who have conditioned them to be too afraid to let them go. On the other hand, they struggle with this co-dependent relationship with their mother.

If you are a son of a narcissistic mother, you may have tremendous cognitive dissonance. You might love and hate her at the same time. You might have extreme rage when it comes to women because you're so angry with your mom, but you might not understand where that is coming from - and that rage is valid. It doesn't mean that you abuse women or blame your girlfriend or daughter or the cashier at the corner store. It means that as a son of a narcissistic mother, you recognize that you have been abused, that you have not been permitted to grow, develop, and attune yourself to what is right. You have not been allowed to become who you truly are. You have had your emotions screwed with. You have been manipulated and toyed with for this woman's agenda, and the anger and rage you feel are valid. That's why it's important to work this out. In psychotherapy, it's essential to work this out with somebody who gets it right. If you're going into therapy, you should find somebody who is well versed in narcissism, especially when it comes to working with the child of a narcissist. Your therapist should allow you to express your anger and rage - to get it all out. You can work it out to be more logical and rational when making decisions regarding your future. It's not your fault if you've experienced co-dependency. Lots of men who have narcissistic mothers find themselves co-dependent. They tend to be the type of men that women walk all over. They are afraid of making women angry, so they attract women who lie and take advantage of them.

Another take on this: some of these men end up with high narcissistic traits themselves. This happens when the mother puts her son on a pedestal and seems very sweet, coddling, nurturing, and all of that. What is truly happening is emotional incest. Mom isn't as overt as another narcissistic mom. She's passive-aggressive in her comments about women and about being left alone. Her message is, *"Don't ever leave me; I have to come first."* So, she might say things like, *"That girl is not good enough for you"* or *"She should treat you better."* But then, what happens could be like a mother-son tag-team. Suppose you're not aware of the enmeshment and the dependency upon mom's approval and how she's manipulating the situation. In that case, you make sure that she's the goddess of your life forever. If you don't know that you haven't cut the cord to mom, then when you attract a woman into your life, there will be a competition, and it will be you and your mother against this woman.

If you are the son of a narcissistic mother, there are so many ways this can play out. If you have an overt narcissistic mother, it might be easier for you to see it, and you might be able to recognize that your mother turned you against every woman you ever brought into the house. She talks bad about everybody - every man, every woman, every child. She infused you with the idea that the world is a scary place because she wants to be the number one in your life.

A healthy mother knows that it's her job to prepare her child for when she is no longer here on planet Earth. Narcissistic mothers don't care; they feel entitled to exploit you emotionally; they guilt trip you and make you feel like you're not making the right decisions; they create guilt and great shame inside you. It is difficult for you to make a decision without your mother, so as an adolescent, she beats you down and insinuates that you're not doing anything right.

That's the overt narcissistic mother, who is easier to recognize. If you want to do things independently, your mother finds ways to gaslight you, insinuating that it is a stupid idea; she finds ways to clip your wings. As you grow up and attract females, you probably find something wrong with every one of them. If you get married, your mom will be a constant source of pain for you and your wife; she will resent your children, she will resent your wife, and she will resent you. When you tell her that something wonderful happened, she finds a way to downgrade it. Her agenda is to get you to worry about her, so if you give her any idea that she is being replaced, there will be an issue.

Once again, it's important for you to recognize that, as the son of a narcissistic mother, you may feel very conflicted and have anger and rage that you are unaware of. Some adult children of narcissistic mothers become people-pleasers and doormats for women. They attract women who are abusive toward them because they don't know how to set boundaries. And it's just a repeat; it's like they marry their mom. Other men take on narcissistic traits when dealing with other women. They felt controlled by their mothers, so their agenda is *"no woman's going to control me, no girlfriend or wife will control me"* because they are dimly aware of how they feel about their mother. They might even hate women. They might still want a relationship with a woman, even sexual relationships, but they struggle with conflict because their mother was such a tyrant.

There are so many ways in which this programming can manifest in your life. You must understand what happened to you in your childhood because it affects you as an adult. You must understand all the tremendous consequences you are suffering. You have been told that life is scary, and when it comes to getting married, there's always a chance that you could get divorced, and there's always a chance that a woman could abandon you. There is always a chance for abandonment issues to manifest themselves and cause you to be emotionally avoidant and unavailable. It's so important that all of us recognize how having narcissistic parents affects us as adults, and we have to heal this gaping wound inside our hearts. We need to allow ourselves to show our emotional needs, but at the same time, we're frightened; we're afraid of being engulfed and enmeshed with our relationship. We need to trust people, but we don't trust people. We need to be loved, but we don't love ourselves.

Given this, you should know that there is help for you. The most important thing you can do is research and understand the consequences of what has happened to you. Understand that you don't know how to set up boundaries with a female or with other people because, for example, you saw your dad beaten down by your narcissistic mother. Maybe you have never seen a man assert boundaries. It's not your fault if you have a mom who puts you on a pedestal, but now you're starting to realize that she created a dependency on you so that you would never leave her and no one would ever replace her. When you become aware of that, you might start to feel angry, and that's normal because you were robbed of your childhood. Your innocence and ability to feel vulnerable were taken from you. Your anger is valid, but that doesn't mean you are now allowed to kick your dog or take your anger out on innocent women. It just means that you are working on yourself. You might need to talk to specialists and psychotherapists skilled in the area of narcissistic abuse and childhood trauma. Moreover, since you have had your feelings completely invalidated and marginalized, it's essential that you deal with a psychotherapist that you feel can be attuned to you.

You have a great conflict inside you, and you have a need as a man to express how you truly feel about your mother in a safe place without being judged. Your friends could claim that you shouldn't feel that way about your mother, or you could have a therapist say you have to forgive your mother. But with the right therapist, you can learn to set boundaries with other people and know that, whether you're in a relationship with someone or not, you are enough. You can learn that you have your identity, that you have a right to be happy and to attune yourself to your innate gifts. So, there is hope that sons of narcissistic mothers will feel heard. It's not your fault; you were raised by a narcissistic mother, and the good news is you can heal. The good news is that you can reclaim your right to a healthy and happy life. You can learn to love yourself and have healthier relationships with other women; you can attract healthy women. You absolutely must know there is hope for you.

2.4 Narcissistic Mothers and Their Daughters

The relationship between a narcissistic mother and her daughter revolves around two dynamics: **manipulation and control**. Under manipulation, the narcissistic mother is constantly making the daughter feel guilty about something. Whether it's how much she's done for her, how much she's done for the family, or how much she's sacrificed, how much she's had to put up with, or how much she's made herself available. The manipulation is always about guilt.

Also, the **manipulation** comes in the form of pretending to care deeply about her daughter. For example, she buys things that the daughter usually doesn't even need at the time. It seems like the mother is completely invested in her daughter, but actually she is doing this strategically as part of the manipulation.

Once the mother gives to the daughter, it seems to the outside world that she's doing this from a genuinely caring place; later on, she can start the guilt trips. That's how the manipulation works, which brings us to the second point of this dynamic: **control**. The guilt trips are meant to control the daughter's emotions, how she feels and behaves toward the mother. They are very confusing to the daughter.

The control shows up in two forms: withholding love and silent treatment. The manipulation first gets the child emotionally invested in the mother. Then, when the child doesn't do what the mother wants at the exact time she expects, the withholding of love and the silent treatment take place. Narcissistic mothers may go even weeks or months without speaking to their children. If the daughter asks for something as simple as lunch money during the silent treatment, her mother may text her that she's so ungrateful. Alternatively, she can withhold attention and care completely, severely neglecting her daughter even if she is just a child. In case the mother still talks to her daughter, she withholds love and affection, living a superficial kind of relationship that is very painful for the daughter.

Narcissistic mothers sabotage their daughters in many ways:

1. Gossip.

Narcissistic mothers thrive on gossip. It is almost their source of energy. The narcissistic mother behaves one way in front of her child and then, behind the child's back, complains and gossips to anyone who cares to listen about her daughter. She says, *"Can you believe what she's done to me after all I've given her?"* or *"Could you believe that she didn't do this?"*

The narcissistic mother sees the daughter as an extension of herself. Narcissists have difficulty seeing people as individuals with autonomy. So, the narcissistic mother sees any of her daughter's achievements as her own as well as any of her daughter's failures. This is where the gossip comes in. It is excruciating for the daughter because she has to hear from family members that her mom is upset with her, while the mother doesn't say this to her face. The mother constantly gossips behind the daughter's back and sabotages her.

2. Undermining.

The narcissistic mother undermines her daughter's intimate relationships. She also undermines her daughter's growth, career, overall happiness, and growth. The narcissistic mother undermines the daughter at every point. For example, she gives advice that the daughter never asked for, especially in intimate relationships: *"Oh my gosh, you don't want to marry now,*" "*You shouldn't be having kids now!*" or "*What about that guy you were dating?*"

The narcissistic mother can be very intrusive. She sees her daughter's relationships as an extension of her own, so she believes that the daughter should marry a certain man even though the daughter doesn't want to. The mother always gives advice, sometimes deliberately to undermine her daughter. In this way, the mother can later say, "I told you, I told you he wasn't worth having a relationship with. I told you that you shouldn't have wasted your time with him." The mother always has to be right, and she always has to make the daughter feel as if there's some sort of flaw within herself.

3. Projection.

Narcissistic mothers always operate in the same way. If you want to know how narcissists feel about themselves, listen to what they project onto you. The narcissistic mother would call the daughter a whore or think that the daughter was surely promiscuous even when the daughter wasn't even thinking about that kind of stuff. This is another way in which narcissistic mothers sabotage their daughters.

4. Playing the victim.

Narcissistic mothers are good at this. They play the victim, and everyone thinks they are martyrs. They say, "*My daughter, she doesn't even come to visit me, after all that I've done for her,*" or "*She won't even stop by and have dinner and check up on me. I can't believe that she's like that.*" To anyone who listens, they are the victims.

They have been gold star mothers. They have been the A-plus mothers to their children, but children are so ungrateful; their children are so mean and disrespectful that they have nothing to do with the mother. In this narrative, the narcissistic mother seems to be a martyr and a victim. This strategy is supposed to invoke guilt in her children, especially her daughter.

5. Triangulation.

Narcissistic mothers make their children feel insecure about themselves and their situation because, in a sick way, that brings them satisfaction. They love to triangulate their children, especially their daughters, with other people to break down their self-esteem. The daughter becomes dependent on the narcissistic mother's approval to the point that she can't even make a decision until she speaks with her mother. In this way, the daughter ends up on the hamster's wheel, always looking for the approval, love, and affection that she has never received.

6. Competition.

It seems counterintuitive to us that a mother would compete with her daughter. Still, most daughters raised by narcissistic mothers will tell you that this competition starts very early on in life. It starts at a very young age, and once the girl begins to grow and develop, the mother sees herself in her daughter. While she's watching her daughter blossom before her eyes, she realizes that she is no longer youthful, or she is no longer beautiful. Her daughter is a constant reminder that her youth has slipped away, and so she goes into competition with her.

Being in competition ties directly into the sabotaging of the daughter because the narcissistic mother does not want the daughter to be any better than she was. She does not want the daughter to achieve anything that she hasn't achieved. She wants to stunt the daughter's growth so that she never outshines her.

Direct competition comes from a place of envy and jealousy. The mother is envious of her own daughter, which is very painful for the daughter. If she doesn't become completely dependent on the mother, she will develop self-esteem and trust issues. *"How can I trust anyone if I can't even trust my mother?"*

If you're an adult daughter of a narcissistic mother, you can turn out two ways: you can either become a narcissist like your mother or be better than that, becoming the most loyal, loving, and giving person anyone has ever known - especially to your children.

PART THREE
NARCISSISTIC FATHERS

BOTH PARENTS ARE VERY IMPORTANT for child development.

Healthy fathers are supportive and make their children develop an overall sense of well-being and self-confidence - improving their cognitive and social skills. All the relationships in adulthood depend on the relationship we had with our father.

Adult daughters will date with people like their father, and adult sons will develop their character and behavioral patterns looking at their father as a model. The relationship between father and children can surely vary, and there is a range of healthy situations. But sadly, some families are driven by sick people: narcissistic fathers, supported by their enabling wives and relatives.

If you are an adult child of a narcissistic father, you grow up living in hell. And since you were born in hell, you could be unaware of how destructive this situation has been for your true self, social skills, and self-esteem.

Before describing narcissistic fathers, we need to consider the structure of a toxic family dominated by a narcissistic father and the roles assigned to the children. These issues will help you fully understand domestic abuse.

3.1 The Narcissistic Father and the Roles He Chooses for His Children

All narcissistic parents assign a role to their children, and this has a tremendous effect on them. They typically put their children in three major roles: the golden child, the scapegoat, and the invisible or lost child.

The **scapegoat** is the child who is *"never good enough."* No matter what these children do, they never satisfy the narcissistic father who always finds ways to make them feel like they have never achieved anything. If these children ever express any anger or resentment towards the father, then he will severely punish them.

The **golden child** is a representation of the grandiose self of the father. The narcissistic father might put all his attention on this child, and sometimes the dysfunctional relationship with the "golden daughter" can even be deeper than the relationship he has with his wife. The golden child is the opposite of the scapegoat child. The golden child can never do any wrong; the narcissistic father idolizes them. He always pays a lot of attention to any tiny accomplishment that this child achieves.

The **invisible/lost child** is the most neglected. The narcissistic father is not very interested in this child. He forgets to do certain things with this child or doesn't want to consider this child's needs. He may forget that the lost child has the same needs as other children.

Let's analyze these situations one by one. Labeling these familial roles can help us gain a broader perspective. Adult children of narcissistic fathers should not adopt these labels permanently, identifying themselves with their role. But we can use this classification to recognize something that we were not conscious of.

Understanding allows us to disengage from the blame game.

The Golden Child

The narcissistic father worships the golden child. This child reflects everything the father wants for himself. Therefore, narcissistic fathers look at their golden children as a trophy. They can do nothing wrong.

Golden sons and golden daughters are not enmeshed with their narcissistic fathers in the same way because the Electra complex and the emotional incest happen only between father and daughter. There is always a fusion of identities, but the son's fusion has more projective contents than the daughter's fusion. For this reason, generally speaking, adult golden daughters of narcissistic fathers are more likely to have NPD than golden sons.

As golden children grow intellectually and physically, their emotions are arrested, and they always feel like they need to satisfy their fathers' wishes and demands. These children are never really able to grow up outside of their fathers' control. Their confidence, self-respect, and identity are tied to their father's approval - so everything the golden child does is based on their father's decisions. If this child tries to be independent, that decision is met with their father's vengeance, even to the point where he sabotages the child's independence, dreams, and visions. He may employ a lot of different tactics: drama, manipulation, control, and lies.

The Scapegoat

The scapegoat gets the blame for the family's problems. The family's burdens and responsibilities are usually placed on this child. If this were you, you might have had the courage to speak out but were bullied, threatened, and dominated back into submission. There are a lot of unspoken rules in narcissistic families, and emotional pain is hidden. There's an undercurrent of competition and sibling rivalry. And it seems like children constantly need to fight for their parents' love and attention.

Narcissistic parents feel threatened by scapegoats because they are the only ones with enough strength and courage to expose family members for who they are. The scapegoat is very sensitive and aware of the truth about what's going on behind the image of the family that the narcissistic parent is trying to create.

If you are the scapegoat or black sheep, you may feel like nothing is never good enough. Your narcissistic father may be happy with you one day and bitterly disappointed the next. If you speak out about how you feel, that perhaps you've been treated unjustly, then your narcissistic father is quick to put you in your place.

The narcissistic father relies on unpredictable mood swings and bullying tactics when dealing with the scapegoat because he avoids taking responsibility for his unfair treatment of his children. You may have always been the one to blame for everything that goes wrong; you may have been picked on and repeatedly put down.

Narcissistic fathers take credit for everything that goes right, but it's the scapegoat's fault for anything that would give a bad impression of the family. This dysfunctional parenting style creates a separation between the children because the father chooses one of them to be the negative example in the family.

The scapegoat is a role narcissistic fathers assign to the most outspoken, extremely intuitive children who are the first to notice a problem.

Since scapegoats are the whistleblowers, they often get accused of being liars, mentally ill, or exaggerating. Of course, outsiders who aren't aware of the narcissistic parent's tactics to control the family believe that. Therefore, scapegoats often feel rejected, isolated, and alone, as if they don't belong anywhere.

The scapegoat experiences childhood feeling burdened with all the faults, wrongdoings, and neglect of the narcissistic parent. The scapegoat tends to act out and unknowingly transmutes all the tension in the family dynamic. This provides a good distraction from what's really going on. If you are the scapegoat, no matter how many A-plus grades you get on your school report or whether you win a trophy or are recognized for your excellent achievements, you are minimized, unacknowledged, or completely ignored by the narcissistic father.

You will never meet your father's expectations. It is impossible to meet his standard, and of course, you will never be as good as his favorite golden child. Scapegoats often carry from their childhood into adulthood heavy feelings of guilt, shame, and not being good enough.

If you are still in contact with your narcissistic father, he continues to imply that you are to blame for all that's wrong in the family or in his life. You may still be the one that the narcissistic father is most ashamed of and disappointed in.

It's interesting to think about the manipulation that's going on. The fact you have been labeled as the black sheep allows all the other family members to start feeling better about themselves. They believe that they are healthier and more obedient to the narcissistic father than you, and again this creates a division within the family.

Another important point is that scapegoat children may fully internalize all their narcissistic fathers' criticism and shame. It means that scapegoats develop this *"inner scapegoating,"* the internal dialogue that constantly reminds them of how bad and flawed they are. It is extremely toxic to a young impressionable child whose identity is still being formed. Adult scapegoat children may struggle with low self-esteem and often continue to feel deeply inadequate and unlovable. They also become super sensitive to any potential signs of approval or disapproval.

Adult scapegoat children also tend to suppress a huge amount of abandonment anxiety because they were emotionally or even physically abandoned by their narcissistic father over and over again.

These are all critical aspects of the profound impact that toxic family dynamics may continue to have on adult relationships. Perhaps you may still have issues with authority. Maybe you're still used to justifying yourself or proving your worth somehow. It's an unconscious pattern that you may still not be aware you are perpetuating because you don't realize how powerful these dysfunctional family dynamics still are.

Once you wake up and understand, you can let go of that label; you can break that pattern by choosing to think and behave completely differently. It's not easy, but a good therapist can help you. You can learn to choose your battles and don't always have to be defensive. You don't always have to feel victimized.

You need to become more self-aware and notice if you are still trying to obtain your parents' approval or validation. Maturing into adulthood means accepting that you cannot have a healthy relationship with a narcissist. You need to process your feelings of frustration, loneliness, rage, and grief.

On a positive note, the scapegoat is the truth-teller. They are the ones who are unable to tolerate lies and injustice. Scapegoats gain tremendous strength because they've survived a lot of criticism and shaming and are used to being threatened by the narcissist. They're also accustomed to being shunned by the rest of the family.

Scapegoats refuse to stay silent and often initiate change. They are the ones most likely to escape, heal, and bring an end to this transgenerational abuse. If this was your allocated role, you could draw a lot of strengths.

The Lost Child

Lost children are often quiet. They have their back up against the wall, don't cause a lot of waves, do pretty well in school, and might even be a bit artistic. Often, the lost child is so quiet that the parents often say, *"Oh, that child is such a blessing; they don't cause any trouble."* There's no big deal, but when lost children do find themselves in trouble, it's serious trouble. Their needs are not being met on any level. It's like they're invisible and get neither blame nor praise from the narcissistic father. This is the child who just seemingly doesn't exist in the family. The basic needs of this kid are ignored across the board.

Essentially, the lost child is alone and finds it hard to let anybody into their private world. There are no natural or easy connections between these children and other people because they feel very lonely and isolated.

They get depressed, but they are also very independent. Since they never felt valuable during childhood, they don't feel valued as adults. As they become teenagers, they feel unlovable and undeserving of trust. They don't even think that their thoughts are worth hearing. Unfortunately, these children may fall into substance abuse, drugs, alcohol, sex addiction, eating disorders, gambling, and other kinds of addictive behaviors.

Since lost children are not used to getting any sort of attention, they don't expect it and don't seek it out in their lives. These are generally not the kids who later become narcissists, but since they become self-reliant, they sometimes have twisted ideas of what life is all about because they came out of a toxic home.

When they leave home, the family will often not even realize they're gone. At school, they might be the kid in the back of the room that nobody speaks to or thinks about. They don't join clubs or groups. These may be the kids who are out back smoking. If they do get involved with others, they're involved with kids like them, the outcasts. It is dangerous and part of the reason why they sometimes get on the wrong side of the law as they get older.

Some lost children choose to throw themselves into school, get good grades, go to the best college, do all the right things, but still never get noticed. These are the ones who are driven by the need for the approval they never got and will never get from their parents.

If you meet a lost child out in the world, they probably appear shy and introverted, but in reality, this person is not just quiet but disconnected from other people. Lost children display this isolation throughout their lives, even when they become adults and get into relationships, which is very sad for them. They are also more likely to read a book or watch TV or play video games or do anything to avoid conflict. They often don't want to deal with others since they don't like conflict. They may also be artistic or musical, and quite often, they're genuinely talented individuals, but since they don't want to be hurt, they're always trying to avoid getting too close to anyone. And if they happen to trust someone enough to get into a relationship, they become dependent and needy.

Unless lost children understand what they're dealing with, if they never get healed, if they never go through the healing process they need, they are in great danger of becoming addicts. But the saddest part of this whole story is that their cycle continues, so they often become the absentee parent or the parent who can't be emotionally connected to their children, which is terrible. Obesity can be an issue for the lost child, as well as anorexia, addiction to the internet or video games. They might become workaholics, but whatever it is, they're going to throw themselves into something, and we just have to hope it is something healthy - which usually is not. The upside is that they do work well alone, are self-reliant, very often quite intelligent, and well-read. If you give them a chance and they get close enough to you, they can become great listeners.

So, how can a lost child recover? The first thing is getting into therapy to get in touch with the rage built up all over these years. There's also a significant amount of fear in lost children because they often have questions and concerns. They have things they want to talk about, and there's nobody to listen to them. Lost children have to recognize the pain of the past. They should acknowledge their core wound and take it to the next level of healing. If you are a lost child, you should realize the emotional emptiness you have carried with you throughout your life and acknowledge that you are indeed lost. Acknowledge that you came out of a toxic home and don't deny it anymore.

Once you have recognized the pain and the situation and own it for what it was, then you can face it. You can begin to form deeper relationships with others and with yourself. You have to get to know yourself first.

If you have noticed yourself playing the victim, it's time to let go of that feeling. Learn to make decisions and set long-term personal goals.

You have to understand that as you heal, you're going to find out that you're not weird, you're not bad, and there isn't anything wrong with you. The fault was just your family and the broken person in your family that caused you to feel like the lost child. You can start healing by changing your perception of yourself and the world around you. If you previously thought, *"If I don't get emotionally involved, I won't get hurt,"* or *"I can't make a difference anyway,"* or *"It's better not to draw attention to myself,"* change that thought pattern. Now begin thinking, *"I deserve attention," "I do make a difference,"* and *"If I don't get emotionally involved, I'll never have meaningful connections."*

You can't allow yourself to be defined by a narcissist. None of us can allow ourselves to be defined by a narcissist because the narcissist looks at us through an ugly, dirty, broken lens. Every lost child on the planet must realize that nothing the narcissist told us about the world was true, and we owe it to ourselves to rediscover the world for what it really is and who we really are - then rediscover ourselves.

3.2 Types of Narcissistic Fathers

Let's talk about narcissistic fathers and how they affect both their daughters and their sons. Narcissistic fathers exist on a spectrum, and this spectrum ranges from neglectful to tyrannical.

Neglectful fathers are not interested in their children's lives. They don't take the time to have quality experiences with their children and are just out there doing something else. Neglected children may not have many negative memories of their father doing something bad, being very critical, or making them cry. But they don't feel like their father has ever been there. They don't have many memories of their father being with them.

Tyrannical fathers are too involved in their children's lives and are extremely controlling. They view their children as an extension of their ego and start something like a military regime at home. The narcissistic tyrannical father puts in place extreme discipline and expects his children to act in a way that he deems right. Children who grow up in that kind of home would be very close to being in prison. It's like being in captivity.

What's especially hurtful, damaging, sad, and tragic about these children is that they grow up without knowing anything else. They may have a friend with a nice dad, make comparisons, and come to see that there are normal families out there. But for the most part, these kids experience the isolationist lifestyle that is common in dysfunctional families.

Tyrannical fathers keep their kids close to themselves and don't allow them to go wandering around and have different experiences. It's like they want to project a positive image of themselves outside the home, but a very different story takes place behind closed doors. Therefore, the message that tyrannical narcissistic fathers send to their children is that what they think of the kids matters the most. And the bottom line is *"I am not good enough," "there is something wrong with me,"* and *"I am not lovable enough."*

Arrogant fathers feel like they are above everybody else, and they have an excessive need to be admired. This grandiosity is characteristic of narcissistic people. Everything they do is for the show; for example, when friends show up for a party at home with the family, these fathers put on this show of charm and entertainment. But when the friends leave and the family stays, it's a very different story. Suddenly, the fear creeps back along with the shame and all those negative feelings that children feel due to so much neglect.

When children hurt themselves and cry to get the attention they need, the dad is absent and doesn't care. There's no empathy. The arrogant father is exploitative, and later on, this will affect the children's lives.

If you are an adult child of one of these narcissistic fathers, you might remember how powerless you were as a child. You depended on him a hundred percent; you had to live in this kind of captivity. Narcissistic fathers need to control all family members to balance their dysfunction, so your father destroyed your boundaries and didn't allow you to define yourself. Narcissistic parents use their children to meet their needs, hurting them if the situation demands it. They hurt their children just by being close to them.

3.3 Narcissistic Fathers and Their Sons

The father has a huge influence on his son's life. There's often a genuine admiration by the son for the strength and the greatness of the father, and there's a desire to live up to the father's expectations. Sons of tyrannical or arrogant narcissistic fathers will talk about many memories they have with their fathers. Even if these sons are in their 20s or 30s, they could still idealize their narcissistic fathers. They may change quite a bit as they realize the true nature of narcissism.

Let's see how a narcissistic father could negatively affect his son.

1. He teaches the son many maladaptive behaviors regarding how to approach other people. One of the areas that stands out here is the father's advice about relationships with women. The father might say something like, *"Women will hurt you, don't trust women, don't let them tell you what you should do"* or *"the man is the head of the household, the man is in charge."* So again, a lot of maladaptive dysfunctional advice about relationships with women. But also, narcissistic fathers have a lot of bad advice about other men, like, *"Don't trust other men; they are just trying to steal your girlfriend or your wife."* They might also teach their son to be aggressive toward other men who are assertive with him. This is common with grandiose narcissism. Essentially, the father teaches the son to escalate confrontations.

2. He has a strong position on whether the son should have children of his own. The strong opinion could be in two ways: have a lot of children or don't have any children. Some fathers say to their sons, *"You should avoid women, avoid marriage, and avoid children to protect your financial assets and sexual liberty."* On the other side, some narcissistic fathers desperately want their sons to get married and have children because they need to boost their grandiosity by carrying on the family name and legacy.

3. He lives vicariously through the son. Of course, we see this with the father-daughter relationship as well, but the effect is stronger in a father-son relationship. This has to do with grandiosity, exaggerated fantasies of power, success, wealth, and ideal love. Insecure fathers who feel like they hadn't had the chance to do a lot of things and had been unable to fulfill their own potential will project their insecurity onto their kids. For this reason, they push their kids to do the things they weren't able to do. If a child is artistic, the narcissistic father might want him to become a football player, a doctor, or an engineer because he has always wanted to do that himself, and he hasn't been able to do so. The son of a narcissistic father always feels like he can't measure up - no matter what he does.

The narcissistic father has fantasies oriented toward the future and the past. If the father failed at school, his narcissistic fantasy is to go back in time or perhaps encounter his teachers in the present and call them losers. Narcissists can do this by showing them how successful they are, and they attempt to use their kids to display this. When Narcissistic fantasies go into the past, they're not about changing the past but adding information to a situation in the past. It's about telling other people something about the greatness of the narcissist and how they missed it.

Let's discuss its implications on the father-son situation. Having a son in school is an interesting opportunity for the father. The fantasies are about humiliating those teachers, and the father thinks he can create a different ending living vicariously through the son. For example, if the son gets a bad grade, the narcissistic father storms down to the school accusing all the teachers of being idiots and not recognizing the son's incredible talent. If his son is bullied at school, the father encourages the son to fight back physically instead of going through the system and reporting the violations. Again, this is to fulfill a fantasy about changing the outcome for the father by living through the son. The son is doing something the father couldn't do in his own past. So again, we see a negative outcome with this type of fantasy going into the past.

The son is a younger version of the father, and the identities of the father and son are merged. The father wants success, wants to fix the wrongs of the past, but he's also unwilling to tolerate a second failure. If the same thing happens to the son, the father would feel all the shame and the pain again. He doesn't want to live this again, so he's going to work to make sure the son has a different experience.

The narcissistic father is a dream-driven perfectionist, and the son can never do enough: if he comes home with a grade "B," dad will say, "*Why not an A?*" After he comes home with an "A," then it will be, "*Why not an A+?*" If he joins the football team, it's going to be, "*Why are you not the captain?*" So it's never good enough, and the son may have that death drive instilled in him.

4. The father is emotionally distant but not necessarily in the way that one might think. He does not focus on the son's emotions but rather on the emotions that the father wants to talk about or wants the son to have. For example, in a school situation, the son might get an A-minus on some project or in a class, and the father might say, "*You should feel terrible about getting that A-minus,*" even though the son might have been happy to get that grade. The narcissistic father is emotionally distant, not because he is indifferent but because he's focusing on emotions that aren't important for the son but on emotions that the son is not really having in the first place.

5. The son may get abandoned for another child who can allow the father to feel more fulfilled. In the beginning, the father may have this messed-up relationship with the son, but if another child with the skills to be more successful comes along, then this child will get all the attention. Sometimes the first son was the initial focus of the father, but he didn't admire the father enough, or the father believes that spending time with this son is a bad investment. Therefore, there's a kind of Machiavellian stick component in the grandiose narcissistic father's behavior.

6. When there is a divorce or a separation, the narcissistic father is typically divisive and encourages the son to take sides with him against the mother. Therefore, the father might teach the son to distrust women. And whether the father gets remarried or not, whether he finds a new partner or not, he often gives up on the relationship with the son. There's distancing and abandonment even though the son didn't do anything to cause that. After a divorce, if the father leaves, he becomes non-custodial, and the father-child relationship tends to erode because of the distance created by the father.

Sometimes, the father puts distance to punish the mother and to punish the son for being loyal to her. To the little boy, the father is a powerful, massive, and invincible figure. As kids, the primary care figures in our lives often appear as gods until we grow up and realize that Santa doesn't exist and that our parents don't know more than we do, and they probably know even less.

Some children can cope well with that. They might be extroverted, very driven naturally, and the pressure from the father might make them do well in their lives even though they are always going to be chasing that approval. But the situation can be tragic if the son doesn't have a sufficient coping mechanism. If he's introverted, wants to paint or make music, then it's going to be very difficult because he's not going to be able to satisfy this father. As a result, he might feel like he doesn't really have a father, which may lead to depression.

Therefore, just like the daughter, the son will never feel good enough; he feels empty inside and inadequate, not having his father's approval. It's a tremendous wound that needs to be excavated and looked at because it ultimately all comes from a lie. Every child is born with infinite value and worth. Life has infinite worth; it's a gift.

When we grow up in a dysfunctional family, we get ensnared in the projection of a sick parent. We get trapped in the lie that we are not good enough. Often narcissistic parents have received this negative perspective from their parents, and all family members are trapped into a transgenerational abuse that is now manifesting in the child.

The son may become a tremendously empathetic people-pleaser to get his validation that way or become very narcissistic and start using people for his purposes while developing contempt for others. This son will never grow up healthy, he will always feel insecure, and it will be very difficult for him to relax and enjoy life.

Life is complex with different outcomes, but often for a child with a narcissistic parent, the possibilities can be narrowed down into two. The child could grow up defeated and resigned to fate; let's call that a beta male. Or he could cope and grow into narcissism; let's call that an alpha male. The son may even go to the extremes of using other people to fulfill his needs, thus perpetuating his father's behavior.

How would a healthy father be for a son?

A healthy father needs to believe in his son and makes his son know that he's proud of him no matter what. But he also gives the child some encouragement to reach his full potential.

Also, the father instills in the son the idea that he's important and that he matters by spending quality time together. A healthy father teaches the son how to be a man by spending quality time with him, giving his child life lessons, talking to him about important things, asking him questions, and letting the child ask difficult questions. If the father also has high moral values, the son will observe and learn by example. Children do remember those moments with their father, and they remember these quality times with their parents.

What should you do if you identify yourself as being a son of a narcissistic father?

First, you need to **accept** it. We can't change the past or rewrite it, but we can reframe it. We can learn to interpret it differently, and we can look at it as lessons for life. Once we have identified the holes, the empty parts within ourselves, we can learn to fulfill ourselves through healthy, positive self-regard.

You have every right to **set boundaries** and cut ties with an abusive father if he continues to behave in this way. In some cases, when a narcissistic father reaches their 60s or 70s, they're a little bit nicer, and they may create a new form of a relationship. But if he's not available and if you feel like he's still devaluing you, then you can just do the minimum to keep things going, or not at all. It's really up to you; if he's abusive, you have every right to set boundaries and cut off contact.

Consider that no matter what you choose, you're no longer dependent on your father, you've got yourself, and you can do well on your own. You can always leave; you can be assertive, realize he is not God, he's not real. He may use guilt or shame to control you — but these are just tactics. Then it will be much easier for you to detach from him. Do therapy so that you can understand what happened and individuate from him. It's essential, and it's like having a second birth in life.

When you go through this process, you start looking at all the patterns in your life, and you get to realize you don't want to be like this anymore. You don't need this person in your life. Take the practical steps you need to individuate and have a second birth. Wherever you are in your journey, just look and try to realize you're doing a tremendous amount of work and be proud of yourself. Give yourself approval and take the time to acknowledge your success.

Analyze your relationships: do you use people? Do you date narcissists? Do you attract people who use you? It's very important to get out of abusive relationships so that you can heal. As long as you're still in that dynamic, it's very difficult to move on, so get out and work on your self-esteem. It's incredibly important because children of abusive parents tend to have low self-esteem.

Keep telling yourself that you are enough. It must become your mantra, even if you may not believe in it fully yet. Keep working on and keep repeating it, and the time will come when your nervous system will pick it up. When that happens, things will start to gain great momentum for you. Use your time alone to invest in yourself and create your life map to inquire into yourself, to have a sense of purpose.

Build a healthy circle, new friends that fill you up, and surround yourself with nurturing and positive people.

The fact you had a narcissistic father doesn't have to victimize you, and it doesn't have to destroy you or make things get worse. It can make you more aware, more assertive, and be a much more powerful individual. That's my wish for you.

3.4 Narcissistic Fathers and their Daughters

When we look specifically at overt/grandiose narcissists, we see that they are extremely confident and dominant in social situations. From research literature, high levels of narcissism in fathers are associated with the tendency to fulfill parental functions very poorly.

Narcissistic fathers typically aren't good fathers in the way most people would define the word "good," but when an overt narcissistic father raises a daughter, she may believe that her father is good in the way most people would think of the word "good."

Regarding psychoanalysis and narcissism, there is something called "*The Electra Complex*." This is when a daughter develops a specific affection for the father with a correspondingly jealous attitude toward the mother. In terms of the signs of a narcissistic father, it's important to note the daughter's role, especially related to how the father parents her. Are there other siblings? Is there a favorite child? Generally, all these questions are important in terms of how we look at the narcissistic father. We see a wide range of behaviors here, from over-involved to completely neglectful fathers. They range from narcissistic possessiveness (toward the golden child) to narcissistic indifference (toward the scapegoat and the lost child). I'm focusing on the signs of the former - the possessiveness and over-involvement with the "*golden daughter.*"

1. The narcissistic father sees the daughter as an extension of himself. His affection for the daughter is there because she is a part of him, and she admires him. This admiration reinforces the narcissistic father's behavior and attitudes. In his mind, he must be doing something right to have such admiration from the daughter.

That's the logic of the narcissist. So, the identities of the father and the daughter become merged because of the father's behavior.

2. He tries to control and shape the daughter into the perfect child. The father controls her money, clothes, possessions, friends, including boyfriends, access to a vehicle and transportation in general, and her time with other relatives. Now, the daughter can interpret this manipulation as the father being protective. She believes that he genuinely and truly cares about her. He cares so much that he spends all this energy controlling her life. So, there can be a sense of pride and satisfaction in having a father who is so attentive. When the daughter of a narcissistic father is asked what she wants out of life, her response often indicates what the father wants, and she struggles to find goals that are truly hers.

3. The daughter's emotional needs are not attended to. The daughter isn't allowed to have an independent personality or express her feelings. The narcissistic father does not focus on her emotional needs, and there is usually a deep focus on other areas of development, like artistic, intellectual, and athletic abilities. The narcissistic father lives vicariously through the daughter. The daughter's success proves that the father has value, so the father needs the daughter to succeed. When the daughter fails, the father is embarrassed, disappointed, and ashamed - and these feelings drive the father to revenge. Usually, he takes revenge out on the daughter in the form of humiliation and wants to make the daughter suffer as he suffered from that failure.

4. The narcissistic father appears to be extremely caring. People see him as a person doing anything for his family and willing to sacrifice for his daughter. Other people may even wish they had a father like him. It can affect the daughter in two main ways: it can reinforce the idea that her father is really doing a good job and he's great, or it can be disgusting to her that people don't see the true nature of her father. When she tries to criticize people for liking her father, they often turn against her and call her ungrateful, leaving her with a sense of isolation and the feeling that nobody can understand her. The daughter learns not to criticize her father, and this attitude may stay with her throughout her life. It can also be evident in her relationships with other men. Often, lack of assertiveness and reluctance to find faults are consequences of a dysfunctional relationship with a narcissistic father.

5. Distorted view of value. The narcissistic father doesn't respect the daughter for who she is; he tries to create his own image of the daughter that he can respect. It's called idealization. The father does not truly see the daughter's value. He only sees what he wants to see. He exaggerates certain skills, characteristics, and abilities and ignores other traits that would have been important to the daughter.

So ultimately, he discourages an interest that could have been beneficial to her. When you seek to make something perfect, you often end up destroying it. For example, if the daughter was interested in playing a musical instrument, and perhaps she has a talent for it, then the narcissistic father may dismiss that. He might say, "*You'll never be famous, respected, or loved for playing an instrument,*" and of course, that's not necessarily true, but that's what the narcissistic father is saying because he has another agenda. He might tell the daughter to focus her time on getting into a prestigious college to study business, or technology, or medicine - and these could be the father's past goals he didn't achieve. Perhaps the father attempted to get into a prestigious college and failed to do that, so in essence, she is his redemption, his opportunity to make things right, and a second chance to wash away the shame of failure.

6. The father is attentive only when other people are watching: graduations, birthday parties, and other social gatherings. He creates good memories for the daughter, times when she feels loved and appreciated. Typically, there will be a lot of photos or maybe even video recordings of these events.

The narcissistic father can manipulate and use his superficial charm to truly make these times special. For example, there may be a school play where the daughter has a key role, and the dad comes early to get a good seat in the front row; he takes a lot of pictures, looks enthusiastic when his daughter is performing but bored and indifferent when other children are performing. Afterward, he tells his daughter that she was the best, and any difficulties she had in the performance were other people's fault. So again, the narcissistic father can be important in terms of forming these memories, and the daughter will rely on these memories when the father is distant, and she uses them to justify her affection toward him.

7. The daughter blames her mother for the perceived flaws of the father. We hear things from the daughter, like the mother didn't appreciate the father for who he was or how the mother didn't understand how great the father was. Or how the father could have reached his full potential if the mother didn't weigh him down. Or how the mother wasn't emotionally attentive to the father and didn't let him be himself or have his own identity. It seems ironic, given the nature of the narcissistic father and his behavior toward the daughter.

In the case of a divorce, the daughter could say the mother drove the father away. All this is understandable because the narcissistic father might have complained to the daughter about the mother. He might have even gone as far as telling the daughter that she shouldn't be like her mother. So, he's pushing the daughter to take sides. When the daughter competes with the mother for the affection and approval of the father, it's the Electra Complex.

So, if you are a daughter of a grandiose narcissistic father, **what should you do** if there are problems that stem from that?

Well, you should try to **build your personal identity**, determining your goals and values. To do this, you need professional help. A psychologist or psychotherapist can help you process your feelings, look at your thoughts and behaviors, and maybe make the changes you need.

I've just described the effects of the behavior of an overt grandiose narcissistic father on his daughters. If the father is a **covert narcissist**, his daughter may feel neglected. It will appear like her needs don't matter. These fathers could be very critical, and it can be overt criticism like, "*Look at you! I don't like how you look; watch what you eat!*" Or they might not even pay you attention. They can also be subtly critical, like, "*You know, I don't want to spend time with you*" or "*You disgust me.*"

These messages can be very devastating to the child's self-image, and as the daughter grows up, she becomes very insecure. She feels like there's something wrong with her. She never got enough, has never been truly seen or heard, and no matter how much she does or how good her accomplishments are, they are never enough, and she's pressed by the father to do better. Sometimes, these women tend to be very successful in their lives. On the flip side, they also tend to exaggerate their looks and talents to get love from others. It could also result in promiscuity, so again, a lack of boundaries. You have an intelligent young woman who is very insecure about her looks and tries to get that love from her father because she feels unsafe and unsatisfied.

These women feel like, no matter what they do, it will always be a lost cause. They could also push healthy people away from themselves because they are afraid of commitment since it's safer to be this way. They may become very good at starting relationships and ending relationships, but not so much at going deep into developing a relationship that requires a tremendous amount of intimacy.

A healthy father would give his daughter a sense of protection and validation, so once she needs help, he will be there for her. He would slowly teach her how to take care of herself and learn to stand on her own and be strong. And if she feels unsafe out there, she can always come back, and daddy will be there for her no matter what. It's like you feel safe to reach out; you feel safe that you could go out there, make mistakes, take risks, and then come back home and feel safe again.

This kind of woman would know how to choose her partners because she's secure in herself and knows what real love truly feels like. Also, she feels special just because she exists. Contrarily, the damage caused by narcissistic fathers to their daughters is very deep and must be treated by a psychotherapist.

PART FOUR
SOLUTIONS

4.1 Effects of Narcissistic Abuse on Adult Children

WHEN WE GROW UP with a narcissistic parent, what we struggle with most is emotional neglect. Narcissistic parents weren't able to do anything more than keep you alive.

In a dysfunctional family home, children learn some habits from a very young age. They constantly hear the following messages, which eventually leads them to grow up and only know some habits they suppose to be healthy.

Change reality to make things look respectable. This brings you up to gaslighting. As a child, you may have seen something that wasn't considered respectable, like your father being drunk and abusive, while the enabling mother says that it didn't really happen. They tell you that's not what you saw, and you shouldn't talk about it with anybody because if you do, they will think you're crazy or won't like you anymore.

Always keep the family secrets. You don't talk about things that you may have seen at home, that you may have seen your parents do. They always want to keep the family secrets, so a child is taught from a young age that they have to protect the family image and always have to talk about their parents in a positive and respectful way. You're taught that if you're loyal and keep mommy's and daddy's secrets, then you will get a reward for that. But if you don't keep their secrets, then mommy and daddy won't love you anymore.

As a child, you always had to act and be like an adult. It is completely unreasonable because you can't expect a child to be an adult. Children in dysfunctional homes sometimes have to parent adult family members. For instance, a child might take care of their father's emotional needs when he has a meltdown. If parents talk to the child about certain adult issues and expect the child to support them emotionally, that is very inappropriate. Sometimes narcissistic parents expect children to do certain chores in the house or take on responsibilities that a child shouldn't take. Narcissistic parents send mixed messages to their children, especially when it comes to relationships. They may say that they love the child, but their behavior shows that they don't care, then the child doesn't know what to feel and has cognitive dissonance.

It's safer to avoid people, not expecting anything, and not to trust anybody. It causes very low self-esteem and codependency.

You are not allowed to feel your feelings as a child. For example, a child might cry because her bunny died, and the narcissistic parent will be like, *"What are you crying for?" "You shouldn't feel like this; it's just a bunny." "It's not a big deal; grow up!"*. The child doesn't know what to do with these feelings and thinks, *"I'm bad because I'm upset because my bunny died; I shouldn't be upset."* Then the child will end up stuffing down these emotions, which will later return and cause anxiety and depression during adulthood.

It's normal that people invade your boundaries because your parents constantly invade your boundaries.

You have to be hyper-vigilant. As a child, you might constantly remember that the world is a dangerous place, that you shouldn't trust people because they might hurt you, and never believe what anybody tells you because they probably want something or are lying. If repeated to a child constantly, they don't learn how to figure things out for themselves. If narcissistic parents are constantly making children scared, saying, "*Something bad will happen,*" then children grow up with no confidence in their own decisions. They are too scared to try anything new because they're afraid of hurting themselves or failing. Children of narcissistic parents learn that they should always be on guard, be over-prepared, and shouldn't trust anybody because they might get hurt if they trust somebody.

You have to be perfect; otherwise, you are not lovable. These parents expect the child to be always perfect. It's destructive because children grow up thinking that their parents won't love them if they don't do something right. As a result, having a narcissistic parent can lead to being unable to take care of yourself, and you are constantly trying to satisfy other people's needs while putting yourself in the background.

Given this, adult children of narcissistic parents usually have the following issues:

1. They often forget their needs and desires. Narcissists always need attention, are arrogant, and manipulate other people because they think they deserve the best.

Translating this into the family context, one of the adverse effects of having a narcissistic parent is that you grow up with the need to please them. In this process, children don't perceive themselves as individuals who have their own needs and desires. Children become a reflection of what their parents want, carrying out all the activities that are expected of them. The narcissistic parent rewards children when they reach the imposed goals, so they learn to seek affection in that way. When they grow up, they have no awareness of their space and try to satisfy others rather than themselves.

2. They have low self-esteem. Narcissistic parents give affection to children only when they want something from them. These parents are so demanding that it's impossible to meet all their expectations. As a result, they send signals or messages that tell the children they aren't good enough. For this reason, adult children of narcissistic parents always feel incompetent, incapable, anxious, and have low self-esteem.

3. They can't love themselves. Narcissistic parents don't allow their children to love themselves and to accept who they are. One of the effects of having a narcissistic parent is having difficulty finding something to feel comfortable with. Even if adult children of narcissistic parents reach big goals or do everything they set out to do, they never feel good enough.

4. They become too helpful. Because of the great attention that a narcissistic parent requires, their children's lives revolve around them, their problems, needs, and happiness. For this reason, children turn into emotionally supportive humans and get involved in situations they shouldn't take part in.

These children take on so many responsibilities forgetting they are kids, to the point of becoming more like a partner. Adult children of narcissistic parents feel they have spent a lifetime solving problems. Although this may be positive - because they have learned to resolve difficulties and be self-sufficient - they carry a great burden within themselves and hardly trust others.

5. They think negatively. Having a narcissistic parent translates into continuous negative messages. For this reason, children treat themselves with criticism and harmful words. There is a mirror effect. Since they have received negative messages from their parents, they treat themselves in the same way.

6. They learn to hide their true essence. Children learn to deny part of their essence to show what the narcissistic parent expects from them. Over time, this process of rejection becomes a habit. As adults, they may have trouble recognizing who they are, their real desires, and what they expect from life and from others.

7. Self-sabotage. Having a narcissistic parent always means hearing the message that you are not good enough. As a result, children always expect the worst from every situation. Growing up, they avoid expressing their emotions to stay as safe as possible. For example, they avoid falling in love, so they don't get abandoned. Naturally, this creates a vicious circle that generates further anxiety and insecurity.

In the next chapters, I will show you some solutions to deal with narcissistic parents.

4.2 How to Handle a Narcissistic Parent

Narcissists purposely provoke situations to gain a narcissistic supply. For example, your narcissistic parent provokes a situation by asking an innocent question, a viewpoint question, or your opinion on something. It's just setting you up so that you give a negative response, which is their narcissistic supply. If your narcissistic parent makes you cry, angry, frustrated, feel bad, they do it to take a hit of narcissistic supply off of you. That's the first fundamental truth you have to recognize.

Once you recognize the truth, going in no contact mode is the best solution to save yourself from narcissistic abuse. But this may be impossible for many reasons, and we must find alternative solutions. If you can't cut off contact, the first helpful thing to do is to avoid giving negative emotional responses, no matter what happens. That's a way to avoid becoming a source of narcissistic supply for your narcissistic parent. So, you're probably thinking, *"How can I do that when they are constantly provoking situations?"*

1. Report physical abuse. If the abuse becomes physical, call the police when you have evidence of physical abuse or when it's happening. Be careful because other family members could support the narcissistic parent, and they could try to gaslight you and deny your version of events. Physical abuse is easier to stop because it's a crime and could be certified by clinical evidence and pursued by the law. Psychological or emotional abuse is more difficult for you because it is not considered a crime, and it's not evident for people outside the family.

2. Learn to set boundaries. These kinds of situations are major lessons because narcissists always push and push those boundaries.

Creating **mental boundaries** can help you drop these negatives while working on your response. You should learn not to take negative comments personally. It is also important to recognize that this person is going to keep touching your buttons. Therefore, it's up to you to do the work and get rid of those buttons. It doesn't mean you have to keep the narcissist in your life just to prove that you've mastered your buttons. It just means you want to do this for your healing.

You can set good boundaries following these tips:

- Never forget that your parent is a narcissist so that you can set reasonable expectations about their behavior.
- Remember that the conversation will always switch to the narcissist.
- Avoid giving away too much information. The narcissist will use the additional data against you. Refuse to be interrogated. For the narcissist, this is a matter of power and control. Claim to be treated like a peer.

3. Reject verbal assaults. Another typical narcissistic behavior is to verbally assault anyone they consider a threat. The adult child of a narcissistic parent may become a target for aggressive, passive-aggressive, or guilt-ridden comments. They can say you are lazy, or your siblings are successful while you are not, or they invested so much in you. If you become defensive, the narcissist has won. Rather, you should ignore the comment or say, *"That's not appropriate,"* and again offer a distracting compliment.

4. Free yourself from victimization. The narcissistic parent plays the victim as a way of guilt-tripping the adult child into submission. To handle this strategy, the adult child has to ignore the narcissist entirely. It is imperative to understand that you might continue to feel tormented mentally and emotionally even if you cut off contact. Sometimes there is such a heavy crushing sense of guilt that you feel like it could suffocate your heart quite literally. If you don't work it out with your parent and cut off the emotional contact with them, somebody else will show up in your life with the same patterns, and they'll touch those same buttons because, inevitably, you have to deal with it.

5. Don't excuse the abuse. These are challenging things to stand up against because you are dealing with a whole family who has been excusing and enabling abuse for generations. It doesn't make it okay that their parents did it to them, and they are victims too. Being abused is never an excuse to abuse someone else, but we can't blame the previous generations. It's important to recognize abuse when it's there and not to tolerate that abuse when you see it. But it's also important to empower ourselves and recognize that this is a transgenerational pattern, and the only way it stops is when we stop it.

6. Reframe the experience. Since you can't change the narcissist, you can reframe the experience: instead of feeling powerless and angry, you can change the way you react to the situation. For example, when your narcissistic parent comes into your room and interrupts you, the first thing that probably happens is you get tense, and your negative emotions arise. Your fight or flight system kicks in because you know that it's not going to end positively.

If you can change and reframe it, you shift your focus to something positive instead of focusing on the negative. For example, you can say in your mind, *"This is an opportunity for me to show to myself that I'm in control of my emotions and that I can decide how to feel about what's going on."* If the narcissist asks you a question, and whatever you answer, they walk away and don't care, then once again, you can reframe that by saying, *"I wonder how many words I'll be able to get out before they walk away."* By viewing it this way, instead of the negative tensions, anger, and feeling of powerlessness coming up, you're viewing it as an opportunity, and you're viewing it in a more positive light.

The narcissistic parent wants to see you in a negative mood in order to feel better about themselves. It's sick and awful, but it's a reality. Once you realize that, you can start taking your power back, refusing to be the narcissist's hit at that moment. Moreover, you don't feel powerless; you feel your own power - a more positive experience.

You can't change the circumstances, but you can change the meaning of the experience by changing your viewpoint into a more positive one, which leaves you feeling better. You will feel empowered and more positive. Reframing is an NLP technique, and it's very helpful when you can't change a circumstance. You no longer want those circumstances to leave you feeling negative, so you can change their meaning.

7. Sudden emergency. Find a valid reason to excuse yourself. A sudden emergency could sound something like this *"That's a good question, but unfortunately, I just got a call from my boss. I have to head back to the office; maybe I'll have a chance later to answer that."* And you leave. Another sudden emergency could be when the narcissist is asking you a question, you're looking at your phone and saying, *"I would love to answer that right now. I just got a text, and I have to do this, but maybe later I can get back to you."*

Or as the narcissist is coming in, if you already know what's going to happen, you could say something like, *"Hey, I'm sorry to interrupt you, but I have to go jump in the shower. I'm kind of in a rush, but you know we'll talk later"* or something like that.

A sudden emergency isn't something you can use every time because your narcissistic parent will catch on, but it's a mindset. Reframing is a temporary solution as well. These are temporary solutions to help you deal with your current situation. Once you're out of being under the same roof as the narcissistic parent, then you can move towards establishing boundaries.

4.3 Protect Yourself from Narcissistic Parents

A narcissistic parent has no ability to show you empathy or compassion. It's a dirty secret because when you talk about it, people who don't have a narcissistic parent judge you, *"It's your only mother"* or *"It's your father!"*, having no idea of what it would be like to have a narcissistic parent. Having a narcissistic parent means that everything is about them: your wedding, relationship, and accomplishments become theirs. Every talent you have is something you got from them, and they are jealous of you. It's super counterintuitive because normal and healthy parents hope that their kids are more successful than they are.

So, let's get into how to protect yourself from narcissistic parents. It is difficult because your inner child wants to be wrong about your mother or father being a narcissist. When you're younger, you just take it in and bring it on yourself. *"If I were better, if I were different, they wouldn't be the way that they are."* But you're not a child anymore, so it's up to you now to take over because your inner child doesn't want to give up.

If your parent is a true narcissist, their ability to love you is minimal because narcissists love you for how they see themselves in you. If you're the golden child, then they get their narcissistic supply from you. They want you to listen to their long stories; they want you to feed their ego and tell them they're right about all the fights they're having with other people.

Narcissists are master manipulators, and the moment you start changing the dance with them, they will notice and start guilt-tripping you. They will humiliate and embarrass you. Narcissistic parents are great at putting up a façade. They're very interested in what people think and are judgmental about you, everything, and everyone.

In order to deal with this situation, you have to first **be in acceptance** because it's only from this place of acceptance that you can start to build a real plan to save yourself. It is urgent that you do this because there will never be enough sacrifice that you can do for your narcissistic parent. There won't be enough feeding their ego, and there won't be enough of you consenting to what they want.

Sacrificing your entire life and happiness to try to please this person, who will be pleased momentarily but not ultimately, is like just bashing your skull against a brick wall. Don't do it. You don't have to, and in the end, it will never be enough for them. They will still want their narcissistic supply from you, and if they are not sucking it out of you, they will be sucking it out of someone else. So, acceptance is the first thing.

The second thing is **knowledge**. You must become knowledgeable about mental illness. Therefore, spend more time learning about narcissistic parents so you can know specifically the type of narcissism you are dealing with. It will also help you feel that you are not alone. You live in a world where millions of people are having the same experience right now.

Whether you are trapped living at home with your narcissistic parent because you don't have enough money to move out, or you're not old enough to move out, or they manipulated you to move across the country to where they lived, now you're miserable because of it. But knowledge is power, so your job is to get super knowledgeable about narcissistic parents.

The next step is setting **boundaries**. It's the most challenging part because you have to take action with the person you fear the most and whose disapproval you are terrified of. But you want to fix the situation.

If your narcissistic parent is torturing you, you've got to draw boundaries for yourself, so if that means limiting contact, stepping back, not picking up the phone and taking a break, then do it. If the situation is really toxic for you and there's abuse, you do not deserve it, and it is your job to protect yourself. If that means cutting off contact, then do it.

If they have any kind of disability, it could be very frustrating. So, the boundaries issue is important, and even though it's challenging initially, you have a right to solve it in the extreme. When you create boundaries with your narcissistic parent, don't tell them anything about yourself and don't tell them about anything that's important to you. If you fail to do so, what you say or reveal will come back later to haunt you. When it comes to a fight, they will just whip it out to throw it at you.

There are other cases when minimal contact can work. Sometimes, we call that "*mitigated contact*," meaning you're very cautious about the kinds of contact that you have with your narcissistic parent. You're very careful about what you're sharing, what you're allowing them in on, and what you're not; you know where the boundaries are set. Since they will always push and push those boundaries, the decision to maintain this contact is ultimately one that only you can make. I can't tell you what is right for you.

Dealing with a narcissistic parent can be so stressful also on your physical health, not just on your psychological health. When your body begins to take on the stress in your mind, the easiest thing to do in the ideal situation is to cut off contact completely. But then there are situations that force you to stay in contact with your abusive parent. So, you have to master your boundaries to externalize that abuse. **If you internalize it, the abuse will direct and control your life**.

You must learn not to take negative comments personally. You do this for your own healing. For this reason, you won't solve the issues with your narcissistic parent just by going no contact with them. Since you have internalized their pathological patterns, you need to detach yourself psychologically and emotionally. It's a hard challenge to stand up against, because a whole family has been excusing and enabling that abuse for generations.

You might need a lot of **forgiveness** to go forward. But you can't force yourself to forgive somebody; you will forgive somebody when you are ready. Sometimes, we get confused around forgiveness and abuse, and we think that forgiveness means saying that it was ok, but it's not. **Forgiveness is not saying that it was OK**. Forgiveness is not condoning that behavior, and sometimes we are afraid that if we forgive, then it means we have to keep that person in our life. It doesn't mean that either. You can forgive that person without ever having a dialogue with them. Your narcissistic parent could be dead, and you can forgive them because this is about you.

Forgiveness is about you, not them. It doesn't do anything good for them. Forgiveness is for your benefit so that you can free yourself from those heavy feelings of resentment, regret, bitterness, and loathing.

Some people can forgive a lot sooner, and it might also be part of their abuse training. They might have been taught to forgive and keep allowing the abuser to hurt them and then forgive again. It's a dysfunctional pattern of forgiveness. Forgiveness doesn't mean you're going to keep turning the other cheek, or you're going to keep allowing the other person to hit you on the head. Your forgiveness is to set yourself free, to release those heavy feelings. It's like sending back to that person all of those heavy feelings they have transferred to you through projection and abuse, which caused you to take on those feelings.

Forgiveness is like the lubrication that sets that stuff free. Your parent's physical presence should have nothing to do with how you feel. If you cut off contact while they are alive, you won't be continually traumatized and triggered every time they continue the abuse. Even after they die, those feelings of imprisonment will still exist inside you until you set yourself free and remember those prison bars aren't real.

They're holographic, but they appear so real. So, you sit in the cage and feel helpless and hopeless, like you can't get out, and then that learned helplessness makes you not even try. You sit in the corner and keep accepting it. But one day, something happens, and you stand up and have this new sense of courage, and you make a run for it and realize that you just passed right through those bars. They weren't even real; it was just a hologram, an image, a cage that didn't really exist. It's your responsibility to stand up and get out of that prison when you're tired of being in there.

The last tip is to **focus on yourself** and put all of your energy into your healing. Join a group or get into therapy because you deserve your own love and attention. Focusing on you also means building healthy relationships with other people. You can find other mother figures, women who are older and are good moms to their kids.

Find a mentor, someone whose energy you're attracted to, a person you feel would be kind, compassionate, empathetic, and with whom you can build a relationship. Part of focusing on you is getting the help you need and deserve so that you can protect yourself and thrive in life.

Another way of focusing on you involves looking for any remnants of your parent that might still be in you. You don't have to become a narcissist, and just because you were raised by one doesn't mean you are one. But you did learn many dysfunctional ways of responding to things, so it would be good if you bring them into your conscious mind and get honest with yourself. Seeing any of those crumbs in your mindset or behavior is part of focusing on you. The next step is figuring out how to remove them, so they don't get any bigger than they already are.

4.4 Protect Yourself from Gaslighting

Gaslighting refers to a situation where someone manipulates you into questioning your own sanity. A typical example is this: you confront your narcissistic parent about a situation and what you think has happened, then you are told what you think has happened hasn't, and you are making a big deal out of nothing. If you confront your narcissistic parent about having abused you, you are told your belief is a lie. So, your reality is canceled, and your perception of reality is overwritten.

The worst thing about gaslighting is the denial of reality; being denied what you have seen with your own eyes and you know to be true; being denied an experience that you know is real. It is worse than the abuse; it can drive you crazy. If you have a narcissistic family, you surely have been gaslighted. Sometimes the victim is not aware of it because they have been gaslighted from early childhood. You can recognize if you have been gaslighted looking at the following signs:

1. You frequently second-guess. You don't trust your memory and frequently wonder if something you think happened did really happen.

2. You feel threatened or on edge around the gaslighter even if you're not aware that they're doing something overtly emotionally or psychologically manipulative.

3. You feel like you're the one who needs to apologize and take responsibility for everything that happens in your family. You often feel like everything is your fault, and everything you do is wrong or bad.

4. You try very hard to make other people feel happy, and for this reason, you feel stressed or overwhelmed. You feel like it's all your fault if not everyone is full of joy. You feel you are to blame, or there's something wrong with you.

5. You feel there's something wrong with you, like you're too weak or too sensitive, or you're flawed beyond repair.

6. You don't trust your judgment, and you feel like you can't make your own decisions. You cannot make a decision until somebody else says what you should do.

7. You feel a general sense of uneasiness. It's not because there's something wrong with you, but because you have been psychologically or emotionally abused. It's important you recognize that you are not broken, and that's a feeling caused by gaslighting.

8. You feel as though you are a weaker version of yourself. You feel you could have been confident, but during the time, you became afraid of speaking up or expressing your needs or feelings because you believe that they don't matter.

Here are some tips for fighting gaslighting:

1. Support your version of events. Trust your version of reality and do not allow it to be altered on demand. Your gaslighter parent will try to bully you, but you will preserve your self-esteem and identity by being defiant.

2. Don't search for accountability. Your parent and their enablers will never take accountability for their actions. Your gaslighting parent will never respond to logic or reason.

3. Don't try to change the situation. Talking with someone who is gaslighting you means you will never feel heard, so the solution is to stop engaging and put yourself first.

4. Healthy detachment. If you try to adapt to a gaslighting situation, your behavior and thinking will become maladaptive. You should distinguish between the world of the gaslighter and the real world.

5. Validate your reality. Let people have their *"alternative facts"* but validate your reality even if it is disavowed. For example, write or paint your experience.

4.5 How to Outsmart the Narcissistic Double Bind Strategy

The double bind technique is a manipulative strategy that narcissists and toxic people love to use. A double bind message is a paradoxical situation in which every choice is wrong and therefore puts the subject in the difficult position to make a decision.

A typical double bind situation is this: if you do something, you'll be punished, but you will also be punished if you don't take that action. You will also be punished if you bring up this difficult situation and cannot leave it. Simply put, action and inaction are both punishable.

The perverse manipulative narcissist uses the double bind strategy to put the victim in a state of confusion, making them feel they are wrong and unable to defend themselves in any case. The manipulator asserts something, then asserts something about his assertion - the two assertions being mutually exclusive. The victim of the paradoxical communication is nailed and unable to get out of the scheme established by the message because whatever they say or do is wrong. This situation is very destructive for a child. The anthropologist Gregory Bateson claimed that being chronically exposed to double bind situations in family relationships may cause schizophrenia.

If you have a narcissistic parent, then you may be a victim of double bind manipulation. So, it's important to recognize and understand how to outsmart this evil manipulation strategy.

Double bind questions are no-win questions: whatever you answer, you are wrong. Let's start with some examples: *"Don't you love me?" "Don't you care?" "Don't you want to make me happy?" "Don't you understand me?" "Can't you even do one thing for me?" "Can't you ever think of anyone but yourself?" "Why do you want to hurt me?" "Why do you always take your mother's side?" "If you really loved me, then you would do this for me." "Why don't you care about your family?" "Is that the way you want to make me feel?" "So, you are basically saying that..."*

Whatever you answer, you will be wrong. So, how can you outsmart it?

You must answer with a positive affirmation about the topic but avoid answering the question. For example, you can answer, "*I really like it...,*" "*I enjoy...,*" "*It feels good to...,*" "*I prefer it when...*" about something of the question's topic.

But the most important thing you should do to neutralize the double bind strategy is to stop thinking that you should care about what other people feel about your thought or your behavior. Stop thinking that other people's happiness depends on you. It's a lie! If you understand that the narcissist's reality is not the real world and his logic is fake, you will be free of manipulation.

4.6 Taking Back Your Power

Adult children of narcissistic parents are stuck in awful relationship patterns. They also feel others take their power away, and that happens time and time again.

Growing into self-differentiation is the process of realizing that, **once you are an adult**, no one can make you feel anything you don't want to feel. There are some situations where we interact with someone and immediately feel intense negativity. Obviously, they're causing it, but we can control our emotional response to it.

The more we are emotionally entangled with someone, the more they can make us feel and think in certain ways. If you have someone in your life who makes you feel guilty or think, *"I'm worthless"* or *"I'm unworthy"* in an automatic way, then you need more emotional distance from them. The more we notice these dynamics, the more we can reframe situations and detach ourselves from toxic people.

So, **how can you gain emotional freedom** and detach yourself from your narcissistic parent?

Think about this: if you didn't invite your parents to lunch every Friday as they always expect, the planets would stay in orbit, and the sun would still come up. The universe won't stop, and they might begin to get used to a new you. Don't get intimidated.

One of the best ways to deal with the *"I'm a horrible child"* situation is to be the *"bad child"* and accept it. Embrace it and challenge the narcissist to do whatever they want to do with it.

You can start taking back your power and stop giving your power away to your narcissistic parent by following these tips:

1. Don't let your emotions run your life. Emotions are important for healing and living life, but if you focus too much on your feelings when dealing with a narcissist, you will be in trouble. Most of your feelings that stem from interactions with narcissists are false. They're not real feelings, and they come out of the relationship system.

2. Analyze your feelings. Ask yourself whether you're feeling a false or an appropriate response to the situation. For example, no adult needs to feel guilty over choosing to do something they would like to do. They're false feelings because they come out of the interactional pattern with your family.

3. Make yourself safe and secure through your own efforts and friendships of your own choosing. If you're financially dependent on your narcissistic parent, work to break that financial dependency. If you're isolated and your strongest social connections are unhealthy family members, begin to build other social networks, support groups, and healthy friends. Change whatever you need to do to build a support group so that you're not dependent on unhealthy family members anymore.

4. Stop negative thinking from playing over and over again in your head. For example, *"My behavior will cause my mother to have a stroke," "I have always been the crazy one," "Everybody in the family thinks I am wrong."* That's not always easy to do, but we do have to resist. Get a reality check from healthy friends, support groups, coaches, therapists, or other professionals. Check to see if you're depressed and if your depression is causing the endless tape to play repeatedly. I mention this because depression can be difficult to get rid of, especially if an identifiable cause of it remains unaddressed.

5. Train yourself to endure abstinence from the love and approval of your narcissistic parent and toxic family members. Go slow because the ability to not care so much about others' love and approval takes a strong emotional backbone. It is critical because we've been addicted to this love, although we've never gotten it. *You are still addicted to trying to get it*, and you might face the temptation of coming back for your fix.

6. Work on self-approval, self-love, and self-care and use your healthy support group as positive reinforcement. They don't need anything from you and don't require obedience or loyalty as the narcissist does; they won't reject you as an unhealthy family would.

4.7 Move Out from a Toxic Environment: Practical Tips

When you move out of a healthy family that encourages their children, you build up good self-esteem. But a narcissistic family isn't encouraging, and it's not supportive. You're constantly being broken down, and you have self-esteem issues because of it. You're repeatedly being told that you can't do things, that you can't do anything with your life, that you're not worth anything, or you're never going to be able to move out.

Narcissistic families are special, so the following tips for moving out will be a bit different from what you would hear when moving out of a typical supportive family. Since you have a narcissistic family, you're going to be met with a lot of resistance when it comes to moving out. In fact, you're taking away their narcissistic supply. I am completely aware of the fact that your guardian has control over you till a certain age. But these tips that I have for you will be from the age of 16, building up to that point where you're finally able to move out.

1. Get a job. Unless you have a large sum of money tucked away somewhere, get a job as soon as possible. If you're looking to move out, a job is literally the most important thing. You must search for a job as soon as you can. I would recommend getting a job so that you can take that job experience with you. If you were to move to a different state or a different city, then you can take that previous job experience and use it to get yourself a better job in the future. If you're still attending high school, I recommend part-time jobs. It doesn't have to be an actual conventional occupation; there are many jobs that you can do online.

2. Replace anything that's not technically yours - especially your car and phone. Replace anything that you are going to need when you live on your own. Your car and your phone are the two most important things because your narcissistic parents would probably want you to give those back as soon as you move out. To avoid losing your car and your phone, when you decide to move out, the first step is to replace them if they are not yours.

3. Find a place. When it comes to moving out and renting out a place somewhere, chances are that a renter will want a guarantor or a co-signer. If your parents refuse to do that and all of your relatives also refuse to do it, you must be your own guarantor. And if you don't have a credit card at the time, you must pay your first three months of rent upfront. So, get yourself a credit card in advance, and build up your credit before you leave.

4. The savings account. It's a sum of money that you have to put for emergencies. Because bad things happen, and when you're left with no money, there's nobody to help you. This emergency account is something that I recommend putting together before you move out. Get a savings account and start putting away a little bit of money. Aspire to put away 10% of your income.

5. Plan the moving process. The moving process is the second most stressful part, because you must get all of your stuff out of your room and into a new place. Depending on how controlling your parents are, that's either going to be hard or quite easy. For this reason, as I said before about the car and the cell phone, if your parents are very controlling, replace everything that's theirs.

Your narcissistic family could use psychological tactics and sabotaging strategies to prevent you from moving out. You can't rely on anybody in the family for help; it's just you on your own.

You must do it by yourself. There isn't going to be anybody out there to help you. When you have toxic parents that don't have any part in your life, you have to do what you have to do all alone. But there's a lot of self-esteem and confidence that you will gain from becoming your own person and making this move by yourself.

When you come of age and know what's best for you, there shouldn't be anybody out there making you doubt yourself, telling you that you're not capable of anything or that you're not worthy enough.

It's totally your decision whether or not you want to cut off contact. You're the person who's in control. That's the wonderful thing about finally being an adult, about finally having the freedom to get away from a toxic environment. You are absolutely 100% in control of your life, and nothing and nobody out there can control you anymore. It is literally the most beautiful and empowering thing you can experience!

4.8 Caring for an Aging Narcissistic Parent

Unfortunately, many adult children of narcissistic parents find themselves having to take care of them at some point in life, because they become old, sick, and have little time left to live. It's such a challenge, after enduring a lifetime of abuse, to take care of somebody who continues to make you feel so much guilt and shame.

Regardless of their age, narcissistic parents always desire to make you feel as if nothing you do is good enough. When they are now dependent, no matter what you do, it is never enough, and they make sure you are aware of that fact every second of the time you spend with them. So, it's very discouraging and disheartening. It just dumps shame on you in an overwhelming way.

The first thing you can do is **separate yourself emotionally** so that you're not constantly emotionally battered. You have to recognize that *"I'm never enough," "I never do enough,"* and whatever thought the narcissist wants you to feel isn't something you can ever fulfill. It doesn't matter if you're awake 24 hours a day, seven days a week. For the narcissist, it still would never be enough. Trying to fulfill the narcissist's demands is like trying to fill a glass with a hole in the bottom. You can keep pouring and pouring, but it will never fill up, and the lack is not on the liquid being poured into the glass. The glass is broken, and that's how you have to view the narcissist.

It's not that you're not doing enough; it's not that you're not a good child or that you are never able to do exactly what they want. It's that they are broken to the point that they will never recognize all that you do. They will never value your efforts, but it's not because of any lack on your part; the issue is with the narcissist. Even though we know this, the narcissist's insults hurt us so deeply because there's a tiny piece inside us that believes those insults. The narcissistic parent may say you're an awful daughter or son, but if you are 100% convinced within yourself that you're a great daughter or son, that insult won't affect you. If you have some doubt, the stain of abuse gets even worse.

So, one of the ways to deal with the guilt is to begin to realize who you are - to see your value not through the eyes of your narcissistic parent but through your own eyes. *"What kind of son/daughter or caregiver am I?"* **Every day find three to four things you do that show you're doing a great job.**

You don't need the narcissistic parent to realize that you're a great child or a great caregiver. The only person you need to convince to heal and not be so ridden with guilt is yourself, and the narcissistic parent has trained you to only find faults with yourself.

The stronger self-image we have, the less the insults and put-downs by narcissistic parents will affect us. If you don't want to be ridden with guilt, you have to get to the bottom of the truth through your eyes, not through the eyes of an emotionally abusive person. You have to train your mind to find who you are in a positive way so that you don't doubt yourself when others doubt you. All this is very important for people with aging narcissistic parents. They have to be with these parents, and they hear a lot of negativity. Having a strong core self-image and working daily on it will help combat those feelings of guilt.

Another thing that will help you is learning how to **manage negative conversations**. A narcissistic parent is always throwing jabs and darts at you, especially when you least expect it. If you learn how to manage conversations, you can avoid getting into another battle. There are some things you can say when your mother begins to attack your way of taking care of her and makes you feel as if nothing you do is enough. When she goes on rants, you can say something like, "*Well, you're entitled to have your own opinion,*" or "*It's such a shame that you view things so negatively, it looks like you're very angry,*" or "*If that's the way you choose to view things, you are entitled to have those views,*" or "*I'm sorry it's so difficult for you to feel contentment.*"

Even if those statements are similar to those used by narcissists toward their children, we need to use them to neutralize their abuse. It's a form of self-defense based on indifference. When narcissists say something negative to take a hit of narcissistic supply, the more you respond to them with negative emotions, the higher they get. In this way, they get addicted to that high, so the next day it will be the same, if not worse.

If you have chosen to take care of your old narcissistic parent, you will be able to do it without being a victim by detaching yourself from their judgment and neutralizing their complaints.

PART FIVE
HEALING

5.1 Complex Post-Traumatic Stress Disorder (CPTSD)

COMPLEX POST-TRAUMATIC STRESS DISORDER is a result of exposure to prolonged repetitive abuse, and this is exactly the kind of abuse you have suffered from your narcissistic parent every single day since you were born. Almost all adult children of narcissistic parents develop this disorder and can only be cured by consulting a psychotherapist.

I want to talk about the five symptoms of Complex PTSD, and then I will dissect them so you can understand what's needed to overcome them. Here are the five symptoms of CPTSD: emotional flashbacks, toxic shame, self-abandonment, vicious inner critic, and social anxiety.

Emotional Flashbacks

Emotional flashbacks are the most noticeable symptom of Complex PTSD. When flashbacks occur, many people don't realize what's happening, and the reason is that emotional flashbacks don't have a visual component. So, it's not like when you have a sudden flashback of something that happened during your childhood, and you understand that you are remembering your past. Instead of a flashback with a visual component, there's only a residual emotion, an overwhelming emotion that overcomes you.

There's no visual component because something happens that strikes your memory, and you don't understand why you're feeling what you are feeling. For example, you're all of a sudden hyper-aroused, your fight or flight system has kicked in, and you're feeling overwhelmed by intense emotions that are far deeper and greater than what the situation at the moment is warranting. That's very confusing.

It's also important to remember that emotional flashbacks vary in degree of intensity, and they also vary in the types of emotions they provoke in you. For example, you might suddenly become overwhelmed with anxiety. You may feel panicky and may not understand why whatever's happening at that moment is provoking so much panic. You might suddenly go into a dissociative state and not understand why you feel very numb and detached in that situation.

Other times, you may react with rage and protect yourself without any apparent reason. You may not understand why you are angry and blowing steam in those circumstances. Often, when you have those overwhelming feelings that don't seem to make sense with what's going on in your current life, it's because you're having an emotional flashback.

The interesting thing with CPTSD is that it doesn't go away until you work on it. It doesn't go away until you recognize that what's happening in your present depends on unresolved issues of the past. We get those emotional flashbacks because of unresolved issues. If you grow up with a narcissistic parent and they treat you horribly, you can't go to them and say, "*Hey, that hurt, and I didn't like that.*" Narcissists never validate your emotions, so you're carrying all of that pain around and stuffing it inside yourself.

Then, even when you're out of touch with the narcissist, it doesn't go away. Emotions are like, *"Hey, now that you're out of that, please acknowledge me, heal me so that we can go on and feel healthy and confident inside of ourselves."*

When you're having an emotional flashback, everything that comes up is because of unresolved pain, circumstances, despair that you felt, and unresolved fear. So, the best way to overcome that is to take the time to recognize all those unresolved things.

As you begin to heal, your emotional flashbacks happen less and less frequently, but until you're fully healed, they may still catch you by surprise. For example, when the overwhelming emotion of rejection is an emotional flashback, you may feel rejected without any reason. This happens because the feelings of being rejected during childhood are still overwhelming for the little child inside you.

Once you know that, you will feel much better. That's the interesting thing about healing from emotional flashbacks: it does bring up pain, it does hurt, it does make you feel anxiety. But you always feel better when you learn how to acknowledge what's going on, validate the emotions that you're feeling, and remind yourself that now your life is different.

For this reason, you should first allow yourself to feel the emotions and don't view them as a bad thing. It's not fun, but it's a step of recovery. You cannot break out of CPTSD and get back fully in touch with yourself until you heal those unresolved issues that are demanding your attention through emotional flashbacks. I suggest you consult a psychotherapist to have support.

Here are ten steps to help you overcome emotional flashbacks:

1. Remember you're safe now. Emotional flashbacks take you into a timeless part of the psyche that feels helpless, hopeless, and surrounded by danger, as you were in childhood. The feelings and sensations you're experiencing are past memories that cannot hurt you. They remind you that you still feel afraid, but you are not in danger and are safe in the present.

2. Have boundaries. If someone provokes those feelings, remind yourself that you don't have to allow anyone to mistreat you, and you're always free to leave dangerous situations.

3. Speak reassuringly to your inner child. Children need to know that you love them unconditionally and that they can come to you for comfort and protection when feeling lost and scared. The same applies to your inner child.

4. Remind yourself that you are in an adult body with the resources to protect yourself.

5. Ease back into your body. Fear may fill your head with worry and numbing, but you can ask your body to relax. You can breathe deeply and slowly. You can slow down, stay in the present, and find a safe place to just unwind.

6. Resist the inner critics. Instead of unfair self-criticism, replace negative thinking with a memorized list of your qualities and accomplishments.

7. Allow yourself to grieve. Flashbacks are opportunities to release old unexpressed feelings of fear, hurt, and abandonment.

8. Cultivate healthy relationships and seek support. Take time alone when you need it, but don't isolate yourself. Feeling shame doesn't mean you are shameful. Educate your friends about flashbacks and ask them to help you talk and feel your way through them.

9. Learn to identify types of triggers that lead to flashbacks. Figure out what you're flashing back to. Flashbacks are opportunities to discover, validate, and heal your wounds from past abuses and abandonment. They also point to your still unmet developmental needs and can motivate you to get them met.

10. Be patient. The recovery process takes considerable time to gradually decrease the intensity, duration, and frequency of flashbacks. Real recovery is a gradually progressive process. It's often a *"two steps forward, one step backward"* situation. So don't beat yourself up if you have a flashback.

Toxic Shame

Toxic shame is important to examine because, sadly, narcissistic parents have their children marinating in shame. Shame is the feeling that accompanies the admission of guilt when you've done something wrong and are sorry. There's nothing wrong with that; in fact, it's healthy. However, it becomes toxic shame when you're no longer feeling bad about what you did, but you're feeling bad about who you are. You don't view your actions as bad, you view yourself as bad, and that's what makes it so damaging. Toxic shame is when you feel as if your core is bad, like you're just dark and evil and there's something wrong with you, and you feel that all the time.

Often narcissistic parents make their children feel shame because, instead of teaching the children that their actions are wrong, they tell them that they are bad. Instead of helping the child to understand that, *"OK, you made a mistake, but you are not a mistake,"* they steep the child in shame and regret. As a result, children never learn how to deal with the feelings of shame that come up. They're just marinating in shame for so long that it becomes a part of their core personality.

Unlike normal shame, which is temporary, toxic shame becomes a part of our self-identity. A person suffering from toxic shame experiences a chronic sense of worthlessness, low self-esteem, and self-hatred, all connected to the belief that they are innately shameful or wrong.

Here are some symptoms you want to look out for if you think you are experiencing toxic shame, especially if you suspect you have CPTSD or have been diagnosed with it:

- You frequently relive traumatic memories from the past that caused shame. You always fuel that toxic shame inside of you by looking at the past and ruminating over it.

- You have a general suspicion and mistrust of other people, even when they try to be nice; you're always expecting somebody to hurt you because you don't think you're worthy of having healthy relationships.

- You have chronic self-hatred and very low self-esteem.

- Feeling chronic unworthiness, you may suffer from dysfunctional relationships with other people.

- You engage in self-sabotaging behavior.

- You have shame anxiety, which is the fear of experiencing shame. It might even be what fuels your social anxiety.

- You feel like you're a fraud or a phony.

- You feel like you have to settle for less.

- You may have an angry or defensive persona; it's your defense mechanism and your fight response.

- You may have a people-pleasing personality, so you are compulsively trying to make yourself feel better by pleasing others. You may also have addictive tendencies in an effort to escape and numb the shame.

Something to remember if you are dealing with toxic shame is that it affects your beliefs about yourself. Your belief system may be very negative, including things like: "*I'm stupid,*" "*I never do anything right,*" "*I'm a bad person,*" "*I'm defective,*" "*There's something wrong with me,*" "*I hate myself,*" "*I'm a failure,*" "*No one could ever possibly really love me,*" "*Nothing I do is right,*" "*I should never have been born.*"

If you have CPTSD or you suspect you have CPTSD, this is one of its side effects, and it's important to examine it from every angle. So, sit down, get out a piece of paper, and **write down your core beliefs about yourself**. Write down how many *positive* core beliefs you have and how many *negative* core beliefs you have. See if they are mostly negative. Go through the signs of toxic shame and see if you exhibit some of them. Once you know what you're feeling, what you're going through, you can work on it alongside a good therapist.

Self-abandonment

Your love has been betrayed because you have trusted your narcissistic parent, and you expected the love to be reciprocal. The most painful betrayal is when narcissistic parents push other family members to engage in self-abandonment. So, let's talk about what self-abandonment looks like in children as well as in adults.

Think about children who receive anger from their narcissistic parents every time they attempt to act as their own individual selves; children who are treated harshly every time they try something new or have a passion for something. Those children will start to feel stifled, angry, and emotionally controlled without understanding why that is happening.

They may not have the mental ability to understand that it is wrong and unhealthy. Commonly, these children turn their anger inward, so they stop doing what they like because it makes their parents mad. Over time, children begin to lose their identity and believe that their only purpose is to please their parents.

For adult children of narcissistic parents, here are some symptoms of self-abandonment:

1. You say yes when you want to say no. If you sense that there's something wrong in saying no, and always feel like you have to say yes, you're abandoning yourself. You're not listening to how you feel, but you're only concerned about how the other person feels.

2. You don't express how you truly think and feel. Maybe you adopt other people's thoughts because you're too scared to show how you feel about the matter. Moreover, you don't speak up because you feel that by exposing your real thoughts or true feelings, you'll be rejected in some way. So, to avoid being rejected by others, you end up rejecting yourself by suppressing your true feelings and thoughts.

3. You settle for less than you deserve. Maybe there's someone in your life who doesn't treat you well, and yet you stay with this person, thinking that you don't deserve better or that this is the life you deserve.

4. Doing what you don't want to do just to please others. Once again, you follow the crowd; you never want to be the one to give a different opinion or follow a different route because of that fear of rejection. You keep compromising instead of staying on course.

5. You allow others to mistreat, criticize, ignore you, or call you names, and yet you are never assertive to put a stop to this behavior.

6. You let fear govern your decisions. Everything you do is motivated by fear.

7. Numbing out with addiction. It could be with alcohol, sex, drugs, shopping, binge-watching TV, or YouTube - anything that allows you to vegetate and not have to focus on your feelings, your thoughts, or anything about yourself.

8. You put yourself last on your list of needs, wants, and desires while you are overly concerned about other people's needs and desires.

9. You judge yourself negatively and have a negative inner voice saying things like, *"I'm not good enough,"* *"I'm inadequate,"* *"I'm a loser,"* *"I'm ugly,"* *"I'm stupid and can't do anything right,"* *"I always make the same mistakes over and over,"* *"I'm never going to be a good person,"* or *"I'm never going to be loved."*

10. You're always ruminating about what others think of you and how they view you, to the point that you never even notice your own feelings. It is not a healthy habit.

11. You make other people responsible for your feelings. Your narcissistic parent makes you feel responsible for their feelings. From this dysfunctional pattern, you learn that your feelings depend on other people. Now you're abandoning yourself because you're not realizing that you don't need other people's validation to know who you are. Therefore, as an adult, it is important to recognize your responsibility when it comes to your feelings.

Other emotional symptoms of self-abandonment are anxiety, depression, exhaustion, unexplained pains, and even chronic illness. So, if you have the majority of the above symptoms and suspect you're in a state of self-abandonment, what can you do? Given that you need professional help to fully recover from CPTSD symptoms, here are some useful tips to put an end to self-abandonment:

1. Be compassionate to yourself. Don't put yourself down on your healing journey. Don't view your healing as the finish line or as the only positive thing on this journey. Every small step toward healing is an achievement. Develop self-compassion.

2. Find out why you engaged in self-abandonment. When did it start? What are you afraid of losing or not getting? Is it approval? Safety? Money? Love? **Write down your fears** and try to get to their root cause. Journaling is beneficial in this regard.

3. Do an inventory of your life. Identify what you need to let go of. It could be a belief you have about yourself or behaviors you're engaged in. What are the steps you need to start doing to let go? Again, writing down the answers can be very helpful.

4. Every day, make time for self-care. Do things that honor you every day. Honor yourself physically. Take care of your body, exercise, eat healthily, and dress in a way that makes you feel happy. It doesn't have to be expensive. Show yourself you're worthy of your own time and attention. Honor yourself emotionally by developing a compassionate dialogue instead of negatively judging yourself all the time. Look for the positive things in yourself. Every day, think of three things that you found good in yourself. Keeping track of it every day, you train your mind to be more positive. Try to look at yourself in a more positive way, notice yourself, and give yourself credit for the positive things you do possess. Repeat to yourself, "*I'm imperfect and yet beautiful just the way I am.*"

5. Write down every day how you feel in your life. What are your thoughts? What are your emotions? What are your desires? What's important to you? The list doesn't have to be too long and could be one or two sentences at that moment. The whole purpose is to start getting you to notice yourself, to be concerned about your thoughts, desires, interests, and what's important to you.

6. Take time to read or listen. It will help you learn healthier ways to think and view yourself.

Once again, if you suspect that you have CPTSD, self-abandonment is one of the features, and it is one you don't want to overlook. Each time we break down CPTSD and work on one aspect of it, it's taking another step forward in our healing journey. As children of narcissists, we were taught that putting the focus on ourselves is selfish and wrong, so we overcompensated by completely abandoning ourselves.

Inner critic

People who have experienced early childhood attachment trauma have a very strong inner protector that they developed to protect themselves from further criticism, ridicule, and feelings of abandonment. Even people with secure attachments can have some of these parts, and that's healthy and normal. What is not healthy, and is a feature of trauma, is when these inner critic voices become very strong to the point that they control and run your life.

In a person who has a history of trauma, their inner critics are not able to just stop with *"Hey, you made a mistake."* They go all the way. *"You are a mistake; you don't deserve anything good, you're always going to be lazy, you're always going to be unlovable and unwanted"* - that kind of thing. So, the critic takes a specific situation and generalizes it to self-worth. If you have experienced early childhood attachment trauma, a part of you might still be stuck in that emotional developmental stage. It means that some situations could still trigger your inner child.

The inner critic that we are talking about considers your inner child immature, out of control, sensitive, weak, and emotional. People with trauma usually have inner critics who hate them and beat them up. Rarely, these inner voices swing to the other extreme, encouraging a high level of self-tolerance and making the person feel entitled to do whatever they want.

There are many types of inner critic voices.

1. The perfectionist. It tells you that you must always do everything perfectly. You should look perfect. You have to be perfect, or nobody will want you. This level of perfectionism can often result in paralysis and procrastination because you don't want to do anything unless you can do it perfectly. Therefore you end up not doing many things because of that fear.

2. The molder. It's very similar to the perfectionist but with a slightly different take. The molder's job is molding you into whatever other people want you to be so that they will like you and accept you.

3. The guilt tripper. It's the voice that says, *"You're bad; you don't deserve forgiveness because not only you made a mistake, you are a mistake."* This inner critic can be prominent and develops especially in situations where there is religiosity mixed in with the attachment trauma.

4. The underminer. This inner voice keeps you from moving forward, becoming successful, and following your dreams because it claims that failure is inevitable. Rather than letting you go out and fail, it tries to hold you back by convincing you that you're not good enough.

5. The taskmaster. This voice tells you that you always have to work harder. You are never allowed to rest, take a break, or have time for yourself just to relax. You always have to be doing something. You always have to stay busy. This part could develop especially in response to parents who constantly push their children to do more, to accomplish more. So, the children always feel like they have to be doing something since their parents don't accept them if they see them playing or relaxing.

6. The controller. This voice controls every single thing you do. It's constantly telling you, *"You're not doing that right, do it this way."* *"You're not putting your clothes on the right way; you're not doing this fast enough; you're not eating the right food; you're disgusting."* Again, it's meant to protect you from the criticism of other people, but it controls your life. It's always telling you that you're doing things wrong and how you should do things instead. This part develops in response to a narcissistic parent who controls every little thing that their child does rather than sitting back and letting the child explore life.

7. The destroyer. This is the harshest inner critic and the voice that wants to crush the life force out of you. It tells you that you don't even belong in this life and that you don't even deserve to exist. While that sounds harsh and almost suicidal, it doesn't always result in suicidal ideation or suicidal attempts. Still, it does develop into a lot of self-punishment and self-sabotaging.

It's important to understand that inner voices are not your parents' voices. They are self-protecting mechanisms. I suggest knowing them as if you are getting to know a new friend. They are there to protect you from your narcissistic mother's pathological behavior. However, they are dysfunctional in healthy social situations. You will see that these inner voices become less intrusive as you appreciate them for their role in your life and process the traumatic events to which they refer.

Social anxiety

Social anxiety can be quite debilitating. It can arise for less than obvious reasons but has obvious symptoms and can greatly affect how we feel. Social anxiety occurs when we interact with others in social situations. It may be on an individual level, or it may be with groups, it may be with people we don't know, or it may occur with people we do know and even with our family members. It's important to watch out for symptoms of social anxiety so that you can be more aware. I will discuss some of them briefly.

1. When you experience social anxiety, you might feel child-like. Social anxiety arises from the past, but some kinds of social situations may trigger your inner child. For this reason, every time you feel anxious interacting with others, you react by displaying child-like attitudes.

2. You don't believe other people would care about anything you've got to say. When you interact with someone, you don't know what to say. You think, "*Why would they be interested in me?*". One possible origin of this could be that you were told to shut up a lot during your childhood, and no one was interested in anything you had got to say. Children and adolescents soak up reality like sponges, so if you are trained to think, "*What I say is pointless, nothing I say is meaningful, no one wants to listen to me,*" then you carry that with you and feel the same way in adulthood.

3. Feelings of unworthiness. You think, "*I'm not worthy of being in this situation, and I am not good enough to be here.*" Let's say in your younger years you were told to go away a lot, or a sibling had preferential treatment over you, or you were humiliated in front of others at home or school. Things like these can cause feelings of unworthiness. When you go into social situations in adulthood, you feel the same way because that's how your brain has been trained. It's how your mind perceives reality.

4. When you're experiencing social anxiety, there's a subconscious feeling that people are evaluating you. For example, you might meet some new potential friends or new people at work, and you feel like they're evaluating you in some way: "*Do they think I'm an idiot?*" "*Are they thinking I look awkward?*" "*Do they think I'm strange?*" It could be an intrusive voice in your mind or just a feeling. Feeling like you are being evaluated or sized up in some way can be a result of excessive criticism in your younger years. Perhaps as a child, you felt like your parents and family members were evaluating you all the time; they were always on your case, and you weren't ever doing good enough.

5. You may feel like an impostor, like *"I don't belong here"* or *"I can't relate at all."* A cause of that could be that you weren't exposed to many social situations in your younger years and are just not used to them. You didn't socialize with many children, had some anxiety, and stayed at home a lot. Therefore, not being used to socializing with others can cause you to feel like an impostor. It's almost like you subconsciously feel you don't have the correct social skills to fit in, and you feel awkward and shouldn't be there. You feel like an impostor for various reasons.

If you've lacked validation, reassurance, and guidance on social skills in your past, there might be confusion as you grow up. Since you've always been on the receiving end of criticism, you now feel as if no matter what you do, it's not good enough. For this reason, social situations can cause you to feel like an impostor.

6. After an interaction, you overcriticize yourself about what you have done. You question how you performed in that social situation. You lack confidence because, during childhood, you received a lot of criticism. In the past you haven't received the support and validation needed to know what is socially acceptable.

7. You may feel intimidated or persecuted. For example, you may find offense where there's none. Humans are largely social beings, and if you've received a lot of intimidation and persecution during your childhood, you can instinctively be defensive in social situations. You feel anxious that what occurred in the past will happen again.

8. You find yourself being a bit of a chameleon in social situations, changing your personality to suit the person you are dealing with. If you are with only one person at a time, it's easier to change your behavior to suit that person. If in a group, instead, it's harder to change yourself to suit everyone in the group to become what you think is more socially acceptable.

9. Physical symptoms. One of these is tenseness in the whole body. Your voice can start to fade, you feel like you should speak quietly, or you end up speaking too fast. You can also end up blushing, not knowing how to position your body. You can appear very tense-looking like a robot because you don't know how to stand or relax your body. You may also experience quick and shallow breaths, sweating, fidgeting, inability to think, difficulty in finding words, stuttering, and an inability to make eye contact.

Many people think that social anxiety is just when you care too much about other people's opinions. But it's much more than that. If a family member has always made fun of you in front of others, you learn that you will be humiliated every time you're in a public setting. Therefore, social anxiety is also fear of humiliation, not only fear of what people think.

Social anxiety isn't always conscious. You might have strong emotions and symptoms and just not know why. You get triggered in social situations because they remind you of something that's happened before. You don't necessarily have vivid memories coming up from your past; it's just that your subconscious gets triggered, so you experience once again that emotion. You feel like avoiding social situations because the subconscious is trying to prevent more pain. The subconscious mind thinks it will happen all over again, anticipates it, and tries to protect itself.

Healing from social anxiety takes time, and you can't just have a quick fix. There are things you can do in your day-to-day life: **conscious work** and **subconscious work**. Doing subconscious work means going back to the memories of what happened to you and using various techniques to heal from those traumatic experiences. For example, you can consult a therapist who uses hypnosis or EMDR techniques.

There are also some things you can do by yourself to recover from these memories. You can **visit these memories in a relaxed state**, because then the subconscious mind is dominant, and you can see them again. This is possible during meditation by relaxing, concentrating on your breath, and then opening your mind to allow memories to pop up in the right way. You could also meditate on the experience of feeling humiliation in a social situation and then try to retrieve a memory of the earliest time you ever felt that way.

It can also help to write everything out so you can have a conversation with yourself on paper. Ask your subconscious mind to take you back to the earliest time you felt that way, and then write out what you're thinking and feeling when memories come up. It's a good strategy to get things out and heal them. If you come across a traumatic memory, you can go into it, re-examine it as a third person, and be there with your younger self. Freeze-frame the memory, talk to your younger self, reassure your younger self, and tell yourself what you need to hear to feel better. For example, if you were receiving some unkind words from siblings telling you that you were worthless and useless, and it was making you feel bad, then you can say to your inner child, "*They don't know what they're saying, they don't really mean it; when they grow up, they're going to be sorry about it.*" In addition, if you say, "*You are loved," "*You are worthy,*" or "*You are wonderful,*" you are keeping it all in the positive - and your subconscious responds to positive commands. Give your younger self a big hug; the key is about going back into your memories. If this turns out to be too painful, don't attempt it yourself but seek professional help to go through it.

Another way to heal from social anxiety is to do some daily work with the **conscious mind**, which will sink into the subconscious mind. You can do affirmations and tell yourself things like, "*I am a strong and confident person,*" "*I am worthy of these social situations,*" "*I have lots of interesting things to say,*" whatever it is you need to hear, talking to your subconscious mind is talking to yourself. So, reassure yourself with whatever affirmation you need to feel better, do it repeatedly in three blocks of 10 times. With time the subconscious mind will accept that. Lastly, talk to yourself in the mirror. You can ask your subconscious mind what's wrong in certain situations: "*Why did I feel that way in that social situation?*" or "*Why am I dreading this social situation?*" and listen to what your subconscious mind says. You might suddenly feel emotions, or you might hear a voice in your mind saying, "*Oh, it was terrible*" or "*I worry that I'm going to make an idiot of myself.*" Talk to yourself or reassure your subconscious mind: "*You're not going to make an idiot of yourself; you're a wonderful person, you're great in everyday life.*" Talk to yourself and reassure your subconscious mind that it is still reeling from the events of the past.

Take a hypnosis session or see a therapist. It's important to get things out and go over them again. Expose them to the light of day with your conscious mind once more, and reason them again with the new understanding you're capable of. Give yourself time; bit by bit, you will feel better.

5.2 Self-healing Tips

Even if CPTSD must be treated by consulting a professional, I want to give you some tips on how to start healing yourself from narcissistic parental abuse.

Understanding and acceptance.

The first piece of advice is to understand your narcissistic parent. Understand why they did certain things, why your parents are the way they are, and why everyone involved is the way they are. Understanding why a certain behavior happens and where it comes from is always helpful. It makes you accept those people's actions without implying that they are right. It also helps you realize that anything you didn't get from your parents had nothing to do with you.

As an adult, you can be logical and understand that wounds came from this, but now you can actually heal. The only way you can heal is by uncovering the wounds and reparenting yourself. It may not be the quickest way to heal from your relationship with your narcissistic parent, but the first thing you have to do is accept them for who they are.

They are incapable of giving, having a real connection, or being there for you. When they do something hurtful or shames you, you can remove yourself from that situation because you know that you didn't cause them to be this way. She would abuse anyone in your place.

It is step number one: accepting who your narcissistic parent is and their inability to be there for you emotionally. If their behavior is too bad, you can choose to cut off all contact with them. Just because we have parents, it doesn't mean we should have relationships with them. When we become adults, we get to choose who is a part of our lives and who is not.

Get rid of negative thoughts.

A lot of the negative stuff playing in your head comes from the relationships that you had with your parents because they didn't teach you how to stay connected to yourself.

Therefore, when negative thoughts come, you have to know that they are part of your programming, and that's the "*I'm not enough*" story you learned from your parents during your childhood. Once you know the origins of your thoughts, you can let them go because that's not who you are. Learning how to monitor and manage your negative thoughts allows you to live a better life.

Stand up to your parents.

It doesn't mean that you simply tell people what you think and what made you angry. Standing up for yourself is being able to love yourself and expressing to others what you need from the relationship. If they can't respect boundaries, alter that relationship by changing your expectations of who they are and what they're capable of.

Reparent yourself.

Being neglected and abused in childhood makes you lack a good internal parent, so you don't have something inside that is directing and caring for you. To heal and function properly, you need to reparent and take care of yourself as if you were a child. You should do it now, or you're going to hurt for the rest of your life. Reparenting yourself is a very complex process. It comes on multiple levels in various ways regarding every single aspect of your life. It starts with being mindful of what's going on and then validating yourself instead of the invalidation you've been getting your whole life.

First of all, you must be aware of what you are thinking and what you are saying to yourself. Secondly, think of comfort. When you think about repairing yourself, think about how a good parent would feel concerning a baby. What did you want to get from your parents? What did you want your parents to say to you that they didn't say? How did you want your narcissistic parent to treat you? That's the first step toward reparenting yourself: learn about yourself and what you need to self-soothe. What do you need to say to yourself that is helpful and encouraging? Think about it.

You can encourage yourself by saying things like, "*You used to do that, but I've noticed that lately you've been doing a little better.*" You must have this inner dialogue that constantly makes you feel better and overcome the older dialogue, which was the negative inner critic from your childhood. Never forget that your comfort matters. Reparenting means taking care of your comfort. You have to start moving through the pain and doing good things for yourself.

A final point on the issue of reparenting: **self-discipline**. Since you didn't get any discipline in childhood, you grew up without an inner parent that is a disciplinarian. If you've suffered that kind of neglect, having discipline in day-to-day life becomes very difficult.

Self-discipline lets you know where to hold yourself accountable as you go through the healing journey.

CONCLUSIONS

WE CAN'T CONSTANTLY LIVE IN THE PAST. There's a wound in you that your narcissistic parent created, and you need to know where the wound is, what it looks like, and how to heal it. Just like any wound, you must take the band-aid off after a couple of days, clean it again, and re-dress it so it can fully heal. That's the kind of work you should do if you really want to heal. It starts with accepting your narcissistic parent for who they are, accepting that they were your past, and working on creating a better future for yourself.

The only way you can do that is by learning to stay connected with yourself, giving yourself those things you wished your parents had given you, allowing yourself to grow up and not be codependent anymore. It might be a very long journey, and you need not be alone. Ask for help, and you will get it.

This book is full of pain but is also full of hope. Even if you were born in the wrong place, growing up dealing with an abusive parent and enabling family members, it is possible to leave the past behind and build a better future by taking control of your life. This book is a painful path of awareness, but it's also the first step of a journey that will take you to the life you deserve.

Never give up, and you will be rewarded! Remember that a journey of a thousand miles begins with a single step. I hope this book will be a good step for you.

Made in the USA
Coppell, TX
08 September 2022

82820506R30085